MEANINGFUL

The story of ideas that fly

BERNADETTE JIWA

Copyright © 2015 by Bernadette Jiwa

Published in Australia by Perceptive Press.

www.thestoryoftelling.com

Portions of this book have appeared previously on
TheStoryofTelling.com blog.

Library of Congress Cataloging-in-Publication Data

Jiwa, Bernadette
Meaningful: The story of ideas that fly / by Bernadette Jiwa
p. cm.
1. Marketing. 2. Business Development. I. Title.
II. Title: Meaningful: The story of ideas that fly

ISBN: 978-0-9944328-0-3

Printed in the United States of America

Book Jacket, Interior and Graphic Design: Reese Spykerman

Book Layout: Kelly Exeter

10 9 8 7 6 5 4 3 2 1

First Edition

For Johnny

We miss you, and that—not the number of years you were here—is the definition of having lived a meaningful life.

CONTENTS

No story lives unless someone wants to listen.
—J. K. ROWLING

MEANINGFUL

The story of ideas that fly

BERNADETTE JIWA

EVERY DAY COUNTS

Our deepest fear is that we will run out of places to hide—that one day there will be no boss who allows us to remain invisible and no political or economic circumstance that stops us from doing the most important work of our lives. We are the ultimate paradox. There are only two things we want—we want to hide and we want to be seen.

I know you're scared that your idea might not work.

I know you worry about being wrong, far more than you celebrate the things you get right.

I know you waste time being anxious that you won't measure up to someone else's metric of success.

I know that some days you say one thing and do another. Why else would the same New Year's resolutions happen every new year?

I know you are afraid people will laugh at you.

I know that every day you walk a tightrope between getting over these fears and creating an impact.

I know you're 'this close' to a breakthrough.

I wrestle with these fears, too. Every single day. On my best days, I put away my nervous laughter, the twenty emails I must answer and my to-do list, and I do the things I don't have the courage to do on the days I want to hide. The things that matter—the kind of things I wish my brother had had a chance to do.

My brother never posted a photo on Facebook or created an iTunes playlist. He didn't ever book a room on Airbnb or make a call from an iPhone. He never got to know what an app was and how magical the Internet would be. He will never walk across the Brooklyn Bridge or eat a moon pie in Gramercy Park. And he won't be there to kiss his daughter when she turns eighteen in ten days' time.

Johnny was the kid who wouldn't come in from playing outside until the very last warning. He lit up any room just by walking into it. Like the Pied Piper, he had trails of friends who followed him and women who adored him (yes, he was impossibly good-looking, too). He was funny and magnetic and caring and genuine, and he died right on the cusp of a brand-new millennium, with a lot of dreams left inside him because he didn't understand that there was no reason to wait for tomorrow to be better—that he didn't need to hide. He was the most magnificent person who had everything he needed, and he didn't know it.

Every day counts.

The two most important things we can do are to allow ourselves to be seen AND to really see others. The greatest gift you can give a person is to see who she is and to reflect that back to her. When we help people to be who they want to be, to take back some of the permission they deny themselves, we are doing our best, most meaningful work.

I see you.

THE STORY OF THIS BOOK

*[F]irst of all, we really need to care about the people we
are designing for, understand what their dreams and
desires and priorities are, and then we have to use that
understanding as the driving force of the work we put
forward, because the second we know what questions …
are important, then all we have to do is answer them.*
—BJARKE INGELS, ARCHITECT

There has never been a more exciting or unpredictable time to
be in business. The Internet has enabled the democratisation of
opportunity by allowing us to find and connect with potential
customers anywhere in the world, and increasingly it provides new
ways to succeed by helping entrepreneurs and innovators to create
value for the people they want to serve.

What I have come to realise through working with companies from
Fortune 500s to businesses run by soloists is that whether we are
business owners, content creators or directors of sales, innovation or
marketing, our working lives are full of opportunities—either taken or,
more often, missed—to create meaning and value for people.

Mostly we're still working in silos and divorcing our ideas and
innovations from our marketing because we are failing to understand
and put first what really matters to the customer. Let me explain.

Typically when we have an idea for a product or service (even in companies with big research and development budgets), that product or service is often created without considering deeply enough what the customer's unmet need is and what the marketing will look, feel and sound like. Early on in the process, we are so focused on ideation and creation that we forget to think about the story we will ask the customer to believe when the product launches, and so we miss an opportunity to make the product or service better. The innovator considers it his mission to create the best app, phone, car, shoe or platform, and then he hands it off to the marketing department to tell the story to the customer. Even entrepreneurs working on their own, iterating rapidly to bring a minimum viable product (MVP) to market, mostly begin with the idea, knowing that they can and will tweak the product based on user feedback down the track.

As I worked with clients, I kept hitting on this same problem over and over again. They were working hard to bring ideas to market and enlisting my help with the storytelling part *after* the idea was fully formed; their first focus was almost completely on the idea itself when it should have been on the prospective user or customer. In fact, it would have been much easier if they hadn't begun with the idea at all, but had started with the customer's story instead. By 'story', I don't simply mean what the customer says she wants or insists she would buy. The customer's story considers not just what the customer tells you, but also what you hear her say, and what you notice her do or be unable to do—things you see her wrestle with or avoid, those that pull her up short and things that bring her joy, too.

The blueprint I am sharing with you in this book helps you to start with the customer's story. This blueprint started out as the seed of an idea when I was working with a global brand to breathe life into their product stories, which began life in the innovation department.

Understanding who their customers were—those customers' needs and their hopes and dreams—became the jumping-off point for both product innovation and marketing.

If marketing is about making people aware of the value you create, to do that, you have to unlock the value in your story. If innovation is about creating value, to do that well, you must unlock the value in the stories of the people you hope to serve.

* * *

Traditionally, we innovate in the hope that our work will find and satisfy an audience because we know that no innovation, however brilliant, survives unless someone wants to use it. But there are no guarantees, and hope is not a business strategy. No business thrives unless it creates a difference for people who are willing to exchange money, time or loyalty for the value that difference brings to their lives. The irony is that while we've been focused on building more efficient factories and platforms to make better products and services, the reason for those factories and platforms to exist has often been put to one side. Behind the closed doors of innovation departments of Fortune 500 companies and in startup garages around the world, many product development teams, entrepreneurs and business owners are trying to create opportunities and products that they hope people will buy and fall in love with (or is that fall in love with and buy?). Product development teams are looking for a technological advantage that enhances the features and benefits of their products and services. Engineers are wrestling with processes, materials, molecules and lines of code, trying to create a breakthrough, often without fully understanding exactly how the end product or service they are working on will fit into peoples' lives, help them overcome a frustration or do more of what they want to do.

What companies and entrepreneurs sometimes forget is that the purpose of innovation is not simply to make new, improved products and services; it is to make things that are meaningful to the people who use them.

The challenge for every company, entrepreneur, business owner and innovator is understanding which ideas will fly and why. The solution lies in following a principle that management consultant Peter Drucker spoke about decades ago: 'the purpose of business is to create and keep a customer'. Drucker goes as far as to say that the customer is the 'starting point' of a business's purpose.

In an era of infinite choices and product parity, if we are to create sustainable, meaningful businesses and brands, it makes sense to start the innovation journey with the customer's story and allow our customers to become not just our target, but our muse.

This book sets out to do just that—to give innovators, product creators and business owners a tool and shared language that help them to understand people and to communicate within their teams and across disciplines *before* they begin. Both the blueprint and this book are designed to help you uncover opportunities and create innovations that match your customers' wants and worldview (which is a heck of a lot easier than trying to change that worldview), and to help your team come together around a shared vision for what the future could look like.

If you are an incumbent brand trying to stay relevant in today's shifting business landscape or a fledgling entrepreneur who is looking for a way to build meaning and value into your business from day one, if you want to understand how to make things people love so that you don't have to work so hard to make people love your things, if you want to continue to do work that you care about and if you want to be proud of the difference your work creates for the people you serve, then this book is for you and you are my muse.

part 1

THE RELEVANCE REVOLUTION

[Y]ou've got to start with the customer experience and work backwards to the technology. You can't start with the technology and try to figure out where you're going to try to sell it ... And as we have tried to come up with a strategy and a vision for Apple, it started with 'What incredible benefits can we give to the customer, where can we take the customer?' Not starting with 'Let's sit down with the engineers and figure out what awesome technology we have and then [ask] how are we going to market that?'
—STEVE JOBS

THE BEFORE AND THE AFTER

It's impossible to write a book on recognising opportunities to innovate and creating ideas that fly without mentioning Apple. While it might be hard to see your business story reflected in that of the most beloved and valuable company in the world (now worth a record $700 billion), and while you might be tired of seeing Apple held up as the gold standard for everything, the way Apple has innovated holds clues for every business. We are used to commentators talking about Apple as a design-driven organisation, but much of this discussion fails to highlight the company's real strength and unrelenting focus. Apple, it turns out, is not in the product and service design business—it's in the customer creation business. Steve Jobs, Jony Ive and Ron Johnson didn't start with the idea for a product; they began by thinking about whom it was for and what mattered to them.

Just as the best stories change the people who encounter them, the brands, businesses, movements, products and services that succeed by being meaningful change people, too. There is a life and a way of being before the product or service existed, and a life and a way of being after it.

Before Apple introduced iTunes, people waited for CDs to be released and shipped. Before Nespresso, people paid for coffee by the jar or went to Starbucks. Before Kindle, we needed bookcases and packed one or two books to take on holiday. Before Wikipedia, encyclopedia salesmen sold thick tomes that would be out of date by the time the working-class parents, who wanted better for their kids, had finished paying for those books in instalments each week.

Before Google—can you remember life before Google, with paper maps, telephone directories, bricks-and-mortar everything and keeping information in your head?

Every successful business creates a new kind of customer. That customer's story changes because the business exists. There is a before-the-product story and an after-the-product story. The change that's brought about doesn't have to be as monumental as the changes that companies like Google create; they can be small shifts in attitude and perception, nearly imperceptible changes in habits that become rituals over time. Enhancing your products or services might signal advancement and feel like progress, but if there is no change in the customer, there is no innovation. What happens because your product exists? Or as author Michael Schrage would say, 'Who do you want your customer to become?'

Before [your product], people did. After [your product], people do.

PERFECTING THE WINGS

There's something magical about the experience of taking a blank sheet of paper and being able to make it take flight with just a few careful, strategic folds. The art of paper plane making has been used for generations, not just to prototype big ideas and lofty innovations—without the humble paper plane, there might have been no Wright brothers' first flight—but also to teach children about engineering, physics, possibility and small miracles. With one or two simple folds, a child learns that her actions can affect her results and that the way she builds something matters.

The point of the exercise isn't to demonstrate the potential of a sheet of paper (although that *is* pretty cool); it's to show the plane maker what her efforts make possible.

Your business is that blank sheet. The kind of plane you build depends on how and where you make the folds.

Success isn't guaranteed even if you make the best plane in the world. John Collins spent three years perfecting his paper plane model, the 'Suzanne', in the hope of claiming the Guinness World Record for the longest paper airplane flight. He did indeed have the best paper plane in the world, but he recognised that he didn't have the best throwing arm. It wasn't until he partnered with Joe Ayoob, a former college-football quarterback, in 2012, that the pair broke the record that had stood since 2003.

On their own, the features and benefits of your products and services, no matter how good they are, cannot sustain your business. It's only when they affect customers in the marketplace that meaning is derived from them. Success is not what you make, but the difference that it makes in people's lives.

Our purpose is not to make the best planes with the perfect wings; it's to make things that enable people to be better versions of themselves— and to show them *their* wings. The best products and services in the world don't simply invite people to say 'this is awesome'; they remind people how great they themselves are.

RELEVANCE IS THE NEW REQUIREMENT

I will never again see the taxi driver who picked me up from JFK airport. He doesn't need to worry about the impression he leaves when he tries to overcharge me for a fraught ride, without a seatbelt in a dirty cab, and he doesn't care if it's me or one of a hundred other visitors that he sees in his rear-view mirror tomorrow. Contrast that with the experience delivered by the Lyft app, which is disrupting the transportation industry around the world by connecting drivers with people who want a ride. Lyft knows when I last booked a car. They know who drove me, exactly how long it took, where he dropped me off and, most important, how I felt when the journey ended and I left my review as the driver pulled away.

When I return to the same hotel for the third time in eighteen months, the people at the reception desk ask me *again* if this is my first stay with them. How is it possible in 2015 that the receptionist doesn't know? She tells me, with a smile, not to forget the 'wine hour'. Free wine for an hour every night before dinner is obviously the highlight of many a trip. So why am I expecting her to know that I don't drink wine and to understand that her comment is completely irrelevant to me?

My Airbnb host meets my oldest son so that she can give him the keys to her apartment to prepare for the arrival of the rest of the family in Sydney the following week. They have a cup of tea together and she discovers that we love good coffee and might use the local gym, so she plots the great coffee places on a map, stocks up on Nespresso pods, and leaves her gym membership card out for us, just in case we feel like using it.

I can roam the floors of Barnes & Noble for hours on end, and not one assistant will make a recommendation to me because they have no idea what kinds of books I might be interested in. Amazon's business model is built on knowing exactly what I want and giving me as many shortcuts to that as possible.

When I was growing up in the '70s, our local butcher knew which cuts of meat my mother would buy on any given day. He knew when we had visitors from England and when money was tight because of how my mother's shopping habits changed. He made a mental note of that kind of information so that he could use it to better serve her, and he did that for every one of his customers.

Ironically, progress, growth and innovation led customers *not* to expect that same level of personalised service anymore. For several decades, while giant corporations dominated the business landscape and monopolies reigned, customers were treated like a homogenous group to be talked at and sold to.

Today there is a shift. Technology is helping us to once again embrace the values of a time when business was about seeing the individual customer. But it's not the technology in isolation, particular platforms or specialised functionality that's driving the change; what's driving this new wave of relevance is the humanity of the entrepreneurs and business owners who create the products and user experiences that people love.

Technology is not just taking us forward—it's taking us back. It's giving us back the ability to better understand our customers so that we can be not only useful, but also important to the people we serve. Upstarts like Lyft and Airbnb are stealing a march on their competitors not just because they have information about their customers, but because they are intentionally building organisations that use that information to create better experiences—ones that make people feel good and give them a story to tell.

As customers, what we crave more than the commodity we think we are paying for is to be understood. What we want more than a reliable ride to our destination, a comfortable bed for the night, or even a book we can get our teeth into, is to really be seen. What we want more than responsive organisations is personal relevance. The value isn't just in the data that businesses collect. What counts is how they use it to make our lives better.

Not so very long ago, the title of this section would have read 'relevance is the new remarkable'. But relevance is what we have come to expect. It's the minimum requirement for doing business now. And the flip side is that you don't always need an app for that.

THE RELEVANCE ENGINE

*The best inventions are never finished. Great inventors
don't just stand there, rub their hands together, and
say 'My work is done here'. They're not Damien Hirst,
freezing their creativity in formaldehyde. They keep
working furiously to create something even better. It's
part love, part necessity. Because if they don't reinvent
their ideas time and again, someone else will—
rendering their life's work irrelevant, or worse still,
extinct!*
—ERIC SCHMIDT, GOOGLE

It's hard to think back to the days when Google was in its infancy and a search query returned ten blue links. What started out as a search engine has become a relevance engine, not just showing us something we searched for, but giving us what we actually want (some would say at the cost of privacy, and yet it's a price we're mostly willing to pay for the gain we get).

What made Google better wasn't the technical ability of their developers; it was how those developers learned from watching what users did and then iterated based on those observations. You probably don't remember the first time you used Google Images, or when and why the product was conceived and rolled out. It all began with a green Versace dress that caused a stir when Jennifer Lopez wore it to the 2000 Grammy Awards. It's not often that a dress warrants its own Wikipedia page (it might have had something to do with the combination of the see-through silk chiffon, the plunging-to-the-navel neckline and the doubled-sided tape required to keep the dress on). But this dress did get its own page, and it did something else: it showed Google that there was a problem to solve.

[I]t was the most popular search query we had ever seen, but we had no surefire way of getting users exactly what they wanted—J-Lo wearing that dress. Our results returned links to websites that may or may not have had the right picture. Or might have described it in the site's text. From that problem, Google Image Search was born.
—*Eric Schmidt*

And so we have been conditioned by technology to expect things to work intuitively. We want the things we choose to use or own to do more than simply be functional, and we demand that businesses we are loyal to put our needs before their processes.

The feeling of being understood by a brand used to surprise and delight us, but we have come to expect it now.

THE THIRD 'A'

Every business today, no matter its size or legacy, faces four massive challenges. They are:

1. Clutter
2. Competition
3. Commoditisation
4. Consumer consciousness

Faced with unlimited choices, savvy customers are becoming more discerning, and more companies are lining up to respond to their wants and needs.

For a long time, product development and marketing were about making stuff and creating awareness and then converting that awareness to attention in the hope that it would lead a prospective customer to take action and part with money.

Awareness and attention were the holy grails of every marketing strategy, so the way you became successful was to pay for more of both. But there's a subtle change taking place. Brands that are starting small, that are customer-centric and not just focused on a single bottom line, are making inroads into territories once dominated by big, established players in the marketplace. People are choosing to spend their money with companies that take the time to get to know them and whose actions resonate with their values—companies that thrive by doing the right thing and by making things customers love, instead of by trying to get customers to love their things. Their advantage isn't necessarily being faster or cheaper, bigger or better; it is that they take time to understand their customer before making what she wants.

Marketing has gone from this…

AWARENESS ——> ATTENTION ——> ACTION

…to this…

ATTRACTION ——> AFFINITY ——> ACTION

It turns out that affinity that is earned, not attention that is bought and paid for, is what's powering business growth now.

THE NEARNESS ADVANTAGE

Twenty years ago, geography mattered. When there was one grocer in every suburb, there was always enough business to go round. Close was an advantage.

It's easy to believe that because digital has dissolved borders, it has simultaneously diluted advantages. But it hasn't; what it has done is redefine them.

Close is still an advantage, but in entirely new ways. Our businesses are no longer constrained by their location and their knowledge of a particular neighbourhood or culture, and they no longer need to rely solely on sales receipts to find out what customers want. Our customers are connecting, interacting and sharing feedback more openly and publicly. The data and feedback they share present an even bigger opportunity to understand them and to add value both to their lives and to our businesses. Today every CEO is one tweet away from her customers. Every Etsy store owner is a click away from another continent. Our online bookstore knows what we love to read, and even our thermostat understands us. We are the first generation of business owners to get the chance to leverage deep understanding of our customers' behaviours, networks, reputations and latent desires to give people exactly what they want—sometimes even before they can articulate what that is. We are the first business owners in history who know what our customers are thinking, feeling and doing even when they are not in our presence.

We know that whoever gets closest to their customer wins, and that's never been more true than it is in a world where entrepreneurship is not limited by the boundaries that domain knowledge, distance or even monopolies once created.

Proximity has taken on a whole new meaning. The places where we feel like we belong may no longer be our neighbourhoods. Where we choose to hang out isn't dictated by our physically being there. For many, digital space has become akin to physical place. And that changes everything about what it is possible to achieve in any industry. The nearness advantage is now open to anyone who cares to leverage it.

DIGITAL IS A GIFT, NOT A SHORTCUT

Everything you're striving for is a by-product of something else— something bigger.

Innovation is a by-product of empathy.

Winning ideas are a by-product of taking risks.

Excellence is the by-product of empowered cultures.

Profits are the by-product of happy customers.

Success is a by-product of mattering.

The tools and the tactics (new and old) that you use to reach your customers are not shortcuts to creating meaningful products and services for those customers.

There's a well-worn business axiom, 'build a better mousetrap and the world will beat a path to your door', but better is not defined by you; it's defined by your customers. And just because they saw your Facebook ad, sponsored update or promoted tweet doesn't mean they cared about it. Just because you reached them doesn't mean you have affected them. Just because they heard you doesn't mean they're listening.

Digital is an incredible medium, an enabler of businesses that previously wouldn't have had a chance of succeeding without a factory and huge investment. But it's not mastering the medium—understanding how the technology works—that matters; it's how and why you use it. You don't have to become the best in the world at Twitter to be the best business in the world at what you do. The opportunity here is far greater than mastering the tools so that we have replacements for the old ways of broadcasting. Digital gives us opportunities to see our customers and to be more responsive to their wants.

Again, though, responsiveness isn't the goal. The result of being responsive is the goal. Digital is a new and valuable route to deeper understanding, a window into parts of our customers' lives that we didn't have before, and it's allowing us not just to reach more people, but also to understand and better serve our customers.

The tools we all have at our fingertips are as much for listening as they are for talking, and the by-product of listening is the opportunity to create something more meaningful and lasting than a 140-character update.

#ME

Tens of thousands of photos with the hashtag #me are uploaded to Instagram every hour of every day. People are showing and telling the world what they care about.

The fundamental needs of humans are laid bare on social media for the world to see. We no longer wear our hearts on our sleeves; we wear them on our Facebook profiles. We can't help ourselves; it's part of our DNA to want to belong, to be seen, to be lovable and loved. We are prepared to trade privacy for significance. But we still want to choose the things we pay attention to and the stories we believe.

When Apple launched the iPhone 6, the company gave the new U2 album away for free to every person who owned an iPhone. The album was automatically uploaded to the user's iTunes account and there didn't seem to be a way to delete it if you didn't want it (that option was introduced later). What the company viewed as a generous gift was seen by many customers as an intrusion. People questioned Apple's right to upload something to their phones without their permission. When Apple did give users the instructions for removing the album, journalists were quick to encourage people to remove it in order to send a signal to Apple about respect. A signal that said, 'You may own the platform, but you don't get to decide what's relevant to me or what becomes part of my story.'

While you have been quietly creating products and developing marketing strategies to make people aware of them, your customer has reinvented herself. She doesn't just want to use what you sell or to have 24/7 access to your platform and be distracted; she no longer wants to simply be sold to or served—she expects to be seen and respected.

THE EXPECTATION HIERARCHY

What's more valuable to your business than attention now is the ability to understand what your customers want. If we think about what our customers want from our products and services as a mirror of Maslow's Hierarchy of Human Needs, the pyramid might look something like this:

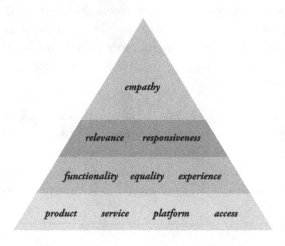

The problem we face as entrepreneurs, business owners and companies is that we get stuck serving the bottom two layers of the pyramid and focus the majority of our energy there. We try to fill perceived gaps in the market and make incremental improvements to what already exists, without fully understanding why our results will matter to customers and end users.

Remember, though, that having an innovation department doesn't necessarily mean you're innovating, for at its core, innovating is about creating something that makes a difference in the lives of users. It has to start with understanding the expectations of the people who will use the product. And what people value most isn't what some companies are focused on delivering.

FOR VS TO

Imagine a world where businesses thought hard about the story their customers would tell about their product before they began to create it. What would the things we make look and feel like if, instead of bringing the marketing department in at the end of the process to decide on a story that will make customers notice what the 'product guys' have built, we created things we knew people wanted, because we fully understood the worldview of those people?

How different would our ideas, stores, websites, product development labs and customer service departments be if we thought about how we wanted customers to feel about our product before we drafted a single design or wrote one word of our business plan?

How could we change everything by creating products for, instead of finding ways to market to, our customers?

CAUSE AND EFFECT

Have you ever noticed what happens at the organic café? As the customer places an order, he asks what's in it. This happens almost every single time.

When we encourage people to believe that something matters, we attract the kind of people who care about that something. Soon buying from us becomes part of their identity—their story. The experience— our posture and products, and the story the business owner is inviting the customer to buy into—is what creates the customer.

In this way, Apple created a new kind of customer by teaching us that design mattered. Lululemon taught us that health and fitness were about mind, body and soul. Patagonia taught us to make caring about the planet part of our purchasing decisions.

The stories our customers believe in shape our ideas, and our ideas shape our customers.

Meaningful products and services—the things we use, come to depend on and learn to love—start life as a set of unfulfilled expectations. A moment of frustration or embarrassment, a feeling of helplessness, or a way of making do. If we approach business and innovation from a place of wanting to fulfil those expectations and meet those needs, then we win. We win by finding wins for the people we serve.

Our job is not to simply obsess about the features and benefits of what we are making; it is to wonder and care about the difference it could make to, or the change it could bring about in, people. Our job, as Steve Jobs put it, is to 'Get closer than ever to your customers. So close that you tell them what they need well before they realize it themselves.'

PERSUASION VS UNDERSTANDING

For a long time we've been conditioned to believe that the key to being great at sales and marketing (and thus to business survival and success) is persuasion.

Will it really matter how much money Microsoft spends on marketing the Surface tablet? Will the Segway finally succeed when we have seen one more advert that tries to tell every person who walks why it should matter to them? Will Land Rover Discovery drivers become convinced to buy a Toyota Prius because marketing tells them it's better for the planet? Is that $8,000 print campaign going to get more people who have never heard of you to trust you and to pick up the phone?

Persuasion once felt like a shortcut. We got very good at telling customers what we wanted them to know, and we forgot to consider what they wanted us to understand. We're coming to realise that understanding our customer and his worldview is no longer the long way round.

LOOKING VS SEEING

Have you ever noticed what a great hairstylist does before he picks up the scissors? On many occasions, I've watched Shane, at my local hair salon, work the magic that makes him a stylist in a million. He listens closely to what the client says she wants and then he takes a step back and really sees her. He's not just looking at the texture, length and colour of her hair; he's seeing all of her.

It's Shane's job to notice the shape of her face, the distance between her eyes and the angle of her jaw. He also has to look for other clues, like her choice of clothing, her posture and her level of confidence. And all the while, he's paying attention to things she mentions that others less skilled might miss, like the story of her son's upcoming wedding and how important it is to look right for the photos. Shane is not just looking; he's imagining what could be, and most important of all, he's understanding how much it matters to the woman sitting under the black nylon cape with water dripping from her split ends.

A good haircut isn't just technically good. It doesn't happen just by paying close attention to each section of hair or the angle of every cut; it's made possible by the stylist's skill in translating what he sees into a style that is not only good but that works for this particular client. The best stylists in the world understand that the tools and the cut are only part of the story.

As marketers, we view our customers through various lenses. We segment them into groups based on their gender, age, income, education, race and occupation. But when we try to see beyond the bald facts of that data and really see them—their problems, pains and frustrations—when we empathise with our customers, understand their circumstances and worldviews and see their potential, we go beyond the need to create awareness of the commodity we made for any old someone and we become the brand that is built on affinity to the particular one. And this, not the number of features we can cram into our products, is how we start to form meaningful bonds with the people we serve.

ATTENTION VS TRUST

Everyone will tell you that in the age of distraction, it's harder than ever to get attention. Actually, that's not strictly true. It's not difficult to interrupt the rock star to ask for a selfie as she checks into her hotel—just a quick tap on the shoulder, fake smiles and you're done. It's easier than ever to spam whomever you want to reach because most people are just an email address and a click away.

If your goal is to get and leverage someone's attention for a split second (even if that someone is the Queen of England), then of course you can. And clickbait can work for a little while.

The kind of attention I think you're after, though, isn't this meaningless, fleeting interaction. It's based on mutual respect and trust—the kind of interaction that's wished for, welcomed and wanted. It's earned and given, not taken; anticipated, not simply tolerated.

The best way to get attention, then, is to give it unconditionally first.

To really understand the worldview of your customers and colleagues.

To anticipate what people need and want. To do things without considering what the payback might be down the line. To create without always calculating what the return on investment will be tomorrow. To stop expecting before caring and to reap what we sow.

To start whispering 'I see you' instead of screeching 'LOOK AT ME'.

We don't have to follow the pack, conventional wisdom or a growth hacking trend of the moment. We each get to choose how we show up in the world and how our businesses are run and our stories are told.

WE DON'T NEED BETTER MARKETING

When I was growing up in Dublin, home baking was the norm. Most families couldn't afford the luxury of expensive, shop-bought cakes, so ironically, something like a mass-produced Mr Kipling's French Fancy was seen as a decadent treat—the kind that was rolled out on a doily when you were having a special guest or a visit from the local priest. Back then, shoppers put complete trust in food manufacturers. The marketing muscle of these companies meant that they were a constant presence in our lives. We encountered them daily through traditional advertising, and we mostly didn't question the truth beyond the story they presented us with.

I imagined Mr Kipling as a kindly old man, a bit like my grandad, who spent his days walking around dipping a spotless forefinger into big bowls of freshly whipped vanilla sponge mixture and painstakingly icing diagonal lines across pink and yellow confections. As shoppers we believed that Mr Kipling made 'exceedingly good cakes' because he told us so during every ad break. We had no way of knowing any different or of digging deeper.

Forty years on and the packaged-cake industry is in trouble. Sales are in decline. Savvy shoppers have access to all the information they need to make informed decisions and better choices. Movements like Jamie Oliver's 'Real Food' campaign have encouraged people to get back in the kitchen and take responsibility for their health. Now more than ever, people want to know what's in their food and understand the health implications of their choices. Raw-food startups, artisan-food entrepreneurs and gluten-free bakeries are popping up to serve this new, more conscious consumer.

On the back of slower sales, the company that owns and operates Mr Kipling (the UK's most popular cake brand) invested £10 million into marketing Mr Kipling in the second half of 2014, bringing us a new package design, an edible billboard, the 'boy shares cake with pink elephant' advert and the 'Life is better with cake' slogan. 'The new packaging will have a modern feel using an uplifting colour palette of pastel colours. The packs will deliver strong appetite appeal without feeling artificial and increase overall shelf appeal and visibility.'

The company invested £20 million at its packing facility 'to double the manufacturing capacity of Mr Kipling Snack Packs', which will be marketed as convenient single-serve items suitable for lunch boxes. Like many food brands, they have added more clearly labelled nutritional information to the front of the packaging because lobbyists and shoppers demanded greater transparency so that people could decide how to make the 'treat' fit into their lives.

The packaging and the slogan may have changed, but it's not clear that those changes are reflected *inside* the box (where it matters) or what investment has been made to improve the product.

Changing the packaging without improving the contents doesn't change the story.

We don't need better marketing. We need better products, made by trustworthy companies, led by brave leaders, who can look us in the eye and say, hand on heart, 'This really *will* make your life better because we put you first.'

THE LEGACY TRAP

I am old enough to remember the news being delivered twice a day. Maybe you lived that, too? My mother sent me down to our local newsagents at 4 p.m. on the dot every day to get the *Evening Herald*. There was always a huddle of paper buyers waiting there for the newspaper delivery guy to scoot past on his motorbike, dropping a thud of string-wrapped, freshly inked copies of the latest news on the ground outside. And that was it—apart from a nightly news bulletin at 6, there would be no fresh news until tomorrow morning.

It's hard to believe that an industry with a four-hundred-year legacy could be disrupted to the extent that the news industry has been disrupted in the first fourteen years of the twenty-first century. The business model that supported the delivery of news to the people has collapsed within a fraction of the time it took to build.

Newspaper advertising fell $40 billion between 2000 and 2013. Even online editions of respected legacy publications like the *New York Times* (30 million unique visitors per month) cannot compete with upstart news websites like BuzzFeed, which boasts five times as many unique visitors and growing.

The decline in the newspaper industry wasn't brought about by a change in the quality of the product. It was brought about by its increasing irrelevance. We've changed how we find and consume information and have gone from being readers and searchers to being discoverers and sharers. You are more likely to be informed of a news event or an article that interests you through someone in your online network rather than from a newspaper. The mode of old news media's delivery, reporting style and method of distribution didn't respond to a new generation of mobile-enabled readers.

The broadcast business model is broken. News media have gone from dominating the authority business to competing in the attention business, and no business can survive there without first considering the customer's story.

Robert G. Kaiser, who spent fifty years as a reporter and editor of *The Washington Post*, explains how news editors traditionally decided what to publish: 'Editors and producers pursued stories that interested them, without much concern for how readers or viewers might react to the journalism that resulted.'

Contrast that with BuzzFeed's focus on the reader; they create headlines for the social sharing generation (50 percent of their audience is between eighteen and thirty-four). BuzzFeed's editors consider not only demographics and social graphs but also how, when and where the reader is consuming content and, most important, what makes her want to pass it on. Because 60 percent of their traffic comes from people using mobile devices and that number is growing, BuzzFeed creates content for the way their readers live, thinking about how to provide articles for the 'bored-in-line network'. If you're queuing for your coffee at Starbucks in the morning, BuzzFeed has you covered.

Legacy industries and brands were lulled into a false sense of security, thinking that their size, reach and scale were enough to maintain domination. Brands that were once unassailable are losing out to smaller, agile companies that have become more relevant because they have the ability to be responsive to customers' needs. Incumbents have been slow to adapt and they continue to try to make people want things, while upstart brands have recognised the power of making things people want.

Tenure is not enough to ensure survival and not just in the news business.

Harry's (the men's grooming-supplies company) has attracted more than 100,000 customers within a year of being in business. That's 100,000 men who regularly buy direct from Harry's and already have an affinity for the brand. The survival and success of this business are not determined by the ability to convince stores to stock their product. Harry's does not rely on celebrity endorsements, and most important, Harry's relationship with its customers is not mediated by a middleman. Since they sell direct to customers, they can tailor subscription packages to those customers, based on their spending and shaving patterns.

Unlike Gillette's, Harry's growth strategy isn't about reaching the most customers; Harry's and startups like them succeed by making the biggest difference to fewer people, and they do this by using new business models that consider more than a single bottom line. As a company, they donate 1 percent of their sales and 1 percent of their employees' time to City Year and other organisations that 'prepare young adults for real-world experiences'.

IMPROBABLE HEROES

Sony, Panasonic or JVC should have been there before him, but they didn't see what Nick Woodman saw when he couldn't get decent action shots during a surfing trip because the camera equipment he could afford wasn't good enough. Inexpensive cameras couldn't get close enough to the action to capture the kind of footage that Nick and his surfing buddies wanted, and the cameras the pros used weren't accessible to amateurs. (You had to be a pro surfer, with someone else out in the water filming you.)

What Nick needed was a wearable camera that wouldn't get in the way and would shoot high-quality point-of-view footage of his surfing exploits. Nick knew that other surfers would want one, too. As he said in an interview with Steve Berra in 2010, 'Every time one of us would get a sick barrel, we'd say to each other: "Agghh! If only we had a camera!" Every surfer knows that feeling!'

It seemed that the most logical and least costly way to start would be to make a wrist strap that could hold the camera in position on the surfer's wrist, but Nick eventually realized that he'd need to create a more durable camera, too, if he was going to find a way to film action sports from the user's up-close and personal perspective. So the idea for his fledgling company went from designing and selling a better action-camera strap to designing and manufacturing the best compact action camera in the world.

Nick started Woodman Labs, did everything himself for the first couple of years, and bootstrapped his company. He put in $30,000 of his own money, his mother lent him $35,000 (and her sewing machine), and his father lent him $200,000.

The first GoPro, which used 35mm film, hit the market in 2004, and the business made $150,000 in revenue that year. The business innovated and evolved to serve its customers, and digital still and video cameras were introduced. Sales doubled every year, and in 2012, 2.3 million GoPros were sold, with the company grossing $512 million.

Go Pro Inc. went public in 2014 and at the IPO it was valued at $2.96 billion.

This is not just a story of timely innovation, success or growth; it's the story of understanding what people want and the willingness to innovate to fulfil that desire. Established brands like Sony, Canon and JVC were better placed than Nick Woodman to bring a point-of-view action camera to market. Why they didn't do it early on, nobody really knows. There are theories. The wheels from concept to market move slowly in a big business with a reputation to protect, revenues to maintain and shareholders to answer to. This inability (or reluctance) to shift gears and act more quickly makes larger companies with hierarchical management structures risk-averse and sometimes less responsive to the desires of the market—real people who are experiencing life in new and very different ways as each year passes.

Sony and JVC introduced action cams to their range in 2012, by which time GoPro had built up massive brand equity in what Nick Woodman prefers to call the 'life cam' market.

The same thing happened in the digital-music-device market, when an incumbent brand and established player in the marketplace was displaced by a newcomer. Sony, which was perfectly placed in both music and the miniaturisation of music devices, missed out on creating what became the iPod. Sony Music was concerned about the loss of revenue due to piracy amongst users who would have the ability to access a wide range of music quickly. The two parts of Sony's business that could have collaborated to revolutionise the music industry didn't, because each was operating and innovating in its own silo. They sacrificed the opportunity to reinvent the music industry of tomorrow, which would respond to how people and the world were changing, because they were trying as hard as they could to protect what was working for the company today.

The 'little guy' doesn't have to start with his company's own story or the current reality of a corporate behemoth. He can start where the customer is, see where she wants to go and build something for a reality that doesn't yet exist. No maintenance of the status quo required.

THE MEANING BUSINESS

Don't compete for the moment. Compete for meaning.
When you do, you'll find that people care because they
want to ... because you earned it.
—BRIAN SOLIS, ALTIMETER GROUP

When I was speaking to my friend Dave about the title of this book (when it was just a collection of headlines in a Word document), he wondered if 'meaningful' was the perfect choice. 'Meaningful' is a word that businesses bandy about every day. We say we need to create meaningful experiences for customers or attach meaning to our brands, and yet we don't always know how to begin creating the thing that matches our ambitions. The word 'meaningful' has lost its potence because it's lived as a descriptor in marketing pitches and staff training manuals for so long that it's become interchangeable with words like 'good', 'great' and 'delightful'. Ironically, the word that should convey so many things has lost its significance, so we need to find a way to bring it back to life.

It's easy to believe that 'meaningful' applies only to the businesses in what some people might call the 'do-good' sector of non-profits, sustainability and so on. But every one of us, from a software designer to a cab driver, is in the meaning business. Without meaning, products and services are just commodities and nobody wants to be in the commodities business.

When the first Apple Store opened in 2001, there was no iPod or iPhone, and 97 percent of people in the U.S. were on dial-up Internet. For every hundred people who visited the store, one person actually bought something. Most people who walked through those glass doors in 2001 didn't own a single Apple product, and the team at Apple were totally comfortable with that, because they knew that if they got it right, success would come off the back of becoming meaningful to people.

That success took a few years to arrive because people didn't understand the stores or the Genius Bars at first, but the Apple Store eventually became 'the most successful retail concept of all time', according to Fast Company. As Ron Johnson, former VP of retail at Apple—the guy we have to thank for the Apple Store concept—said, 'People really love our stores because we are more than a store; we are a place to belong.'

And one by one we did feel like we belonged. We fell in love with the idea of buying something that didn't just work, but felt good to own because of the meaning we had attached to it. Apple didn't become the most beloved brand in the world by making beautiful stuff; they got there by making sense of what the future would look like and by making meaning for the people who would live in that future.

part 2

THE FUTURE STARTS HERE

*The future belongs to a very different kind of person
with a very different kind of mind—creators and
empathizers, pattern recognizers, and meaning makers.*
—DANIEL PINK, *A WHOLE NEW MIND:
WHY RIGHT-BRAINERS WILL RULE THE FUTURE*

THE DONE THING

It's 2 p.m. on Christmas Eve and the throng of men who knocked off early to finish (or start) their last-minute shopping is three deep along all sides of the perfume counter. They are doing what's expected, what feels safe and unobjectionable. They are acting on an assumption they have been conditioned to believe is true. Just as nobody ever got fired for hiring McKinsey to give business advice, no man was ever rejected for handing over a nicely wrapped bottle of perfume on Christmas day.

A lot of business ideas are born from the same mentality. We make assumptions about what people want based on what we think we know to be true, rather than on what could be. We resist trying to deviate too far from the expected norms because the price of failure feels too high. We choose safety over the extraordinary. We do *the done thing* because that's what has the least chance of being an outright failure. Building on what's been done before feels less risky. The irony is that the unremarkable and familiar thing also has the least chance of being a runaway success.

Once upon a time, taking photos using rolls of photographic film was *the done thing*, as were using keypads that took up 40 percent of the front of your mobile phone and having to return a rented DVD by 6 p.m. the following day. What's meaningful today can become meaningless tomorrow, not because it no longer works but because what people believe and how they think, act and feel change. The context surrounding what works is in sync with the beliefs and behaviours of the people who support it. As businesspeople, innovators, artists and creators, we have two choices. We can simply keep giving customers what works today, or we can make it our business to understand where those people we serve want to go and take them there.

WHERE IS THE ARCHITECTURE?

My son is in his final year as an architecture and design student. He was excited to complete an assignment to reimagine how an old department-store building could be repurposed to serve a community that he cares about. We spoke on the phone and batted ideas back and forth; he researched other similar projects and thought a lot about what was unique about the community the building would serve, how its members might use it and how it could best serve them. In his first meeting with his tutor after this initial research period, she had one question and criticism for him.

'You have not drawn a single thing; where is the architecture?'

He was crushed. What he wanted to communicate (but couldn't, unless he doesn't want to graduate any time soon) was this: we need to put down the pencil and start with the people. The people are the architecture—they are the foundation and framework for everything we build. The people will shape the character of the building. Without them, there is no reason for walls or windows to exist, no need to think about when the sun rises, where the light will fall or what the orientation of a certain room should be. If we are to build anything useful or significant—a place where people feel like they belong—we have to spend twice as much time thinking about them as we do in front of our CAD drawings.

It's why we build, not what we build, that matters.

DISRUPTION HAPPENS ONE PERSON AT A TIME

The best—maybe the only?—real, direct measure of
'innovation' is change in human behaviour.
—STEWART BUTTERFIELD, CEO, SLACK

The truth about disruptive innovations isn't that they disrupt industries, but that they disrupt people's lives for the better. Any innovation that is adopted or idea that spreads succeeds because enough people want the change that happens as a result. Success doesn't come from simply making things that work—it is born from changing the story of the user or customer for the better.

Take the practice of shaving, as an example. Without shaving implements, our ancestors were a hairy bunch. There are cave drawings to suggest that even our prehistoric forebears used stones, shells and pieces of flint to shave and groom themselves.

Although ancient Egyptians were the real shaving pioneers, using implements forged from metal, the more practical advantages of grooming became more apparent around 300 BCE when soldiers from the Greek and Roman armies began shaving to prevent their hair and beards from being grabbed by their enemies in hand-to-hand combat. Their hairy and unkempt enemies became known as 'the barbarians' because of their unbarbered state.

Cutthroat-style shaving implements changed little until the eighteenth century, when Jean-Jacques Perret invented the safety razor. But it wasn't until 1895 that shaving rituals changed dramatically when King Camp Gillette designed and marketed a razor that didn't need sharpening. Gillette saw an opportunity to create a razor with blades that could be replaced when they became dull. The manufacture of these blades wasn't straightforward and it took two years from filing patents for Gillette to get his disposable blades to market.

This finally happened in 1903, when Gillette sold a grand total of 51 razors and 168 blades. Within two years, sales rose dramatically to 90,000 razors and 2.5 million blades. By 1908, Gillette was selling 300,000 razors and 14 million blades, traditional barbering services were losing business and men's morning ritual had changed forever.

There can be no question that King Camp Gillette was one of the most successful entrepreneurs of his time. He created a product and business model that would dominate an industry for more than a century. Today, Gillette sales total $8 billion and the brand is valued at $19 billion, making it the twenty-seventh most valuable brand in the world.

It has taken more than a hundred years, but once again the shaving business model is being disrupted, and established brands like Gillette are being challenged by startups offering cheaper subscription razor services. They are starting small, converting one man at a time. Just as King Camp Gillette did.

SHIFTS DON'T HAPPEN BY ACCIDENT

My three boys look at twenty-year-old technology (stuff that's about as old as they are) and laugh at how 'rubbish' it was. They snort at how big, clunky, unintuitive, disconnected and awkward the music players and phones of old were. We all wonder when human-centred design became not just fashionable but a must. Shifts don't simply happen by accident; they are created with intention when technology and innovation collide with and change our cultural expectations and desires. We design the future by interpreting how today's story might unfold tomorrow. The things that survive and thrive do so because they fit within our evolving storylines.

It can be hard to remember a previous norm once we transition away from it, but the switch from waiting for the Top 40 CDs to arrive at the record store once a week to downloading a song in seconds from iTunes didn't happen overnight, even though sometimes it feels that way. Innovation changes our expectations, and our expectations change innovation.

Think about the massive shifts that have happened in every industry in the last two decades—all of them enabled by the digital revolution and our exponential connectedness.

Transportation

The shift in cultural and behavioural norms regarding how we get (ourselves and stuff) from point A to point B have been fascinating to watch. We are now happy to think less about ownership and more about sharing and outsourcing, using transportation and delivery services like Lyft, Zipcar and Postmates. And we don't want to hope that we can hail a cab at the end of the street; we want to know that the driver is on his way, where he is right now and how long it will take him to get here. Yes, of course there is an app for that. There is also one called Waze that helps you to avoid traffic jams and accidents in real time, and there is a slew of on-demand delivery services.

These innovations are a classic case of capability finally catching up with peoples' deep-seated desires. We don't just want to get from here to there; we want to eliminate the uncertainties that used to be part of the journey.

Music

The seeds of the ideas for the iPod and iTunes were sown long before the technological capability to create them existed. How we personalise our music today, using playlists, has its origins in the mix tapes of the '70s. It seems obvious now that, even following several iterations of innovation, from vinyl to tapes and then CDs, people would grow tired of buying a full album for the one hit song they loved and of playing full albums from single artists on personal CD music players. However, the size, convenience and portability of those clunky, last-century devices weren't the whole basis for the innovation story. At its core, iTunes was created in response to people's deep-seated desire to personalise things.

The revolution in the music industry was about more than the need to find a way to make people pay for music, which was becoming easier to illegally download and own for free. It was about giving people what they had wanted all along: the songs that mattered to them.

Shopping

It was inevitable that shopping for anything you can care to mention would shift from local to global with the advent of the Internet. We've become so used to getting what we want when we want it that rummaging through racks of clothes hangers for the right size in a physical store seems almost Neolithic. One of the big business trends for 2015 is the growth of the on-demand business sector. Our unwillingness to wait in the digital world is now manifesting in the physical world. Queuing and waiting are fast becoming things of the past. Inconvenience is being wiped from our lives and our vocabularies. Shopping is no longer about getting what we need and want; it's about instant gratification.

Publishing

Traditional book sales have plummeted in half a decade. Print-book sales fell 9 percent in 2012. In the UK alone, digital books make up 30 percent of the market, with ebook sales doubling between 2011 and 2014. When Amazon launched the Kindle e-reader in 2007, they changed how we read, who has the power to publish and how we perceive the value of books. Amazon made more books more accessible to everyone.

Books used to compete only with other pastimes and analogue publications; now they compete with digital infinity. In 2010, Eric Schmidt pointed out that we now create as much information in two days as we did from the dawn of civilization up until 2003. Who knows what the comparison will be five years from now? If we are going to invest hours of our time, we need to know that the book will be worth reading, because there are plenty of alternatives.

Physical Environment

What would the world look like if we could optimise our homes to be responsive to how we use them? Making our environments respond to the rhythm of our lives makes perfect sense. Even if they live in identical houses, no two families are alike; it seems reasonable, then, that our environments should adapt to what happens around and within them. That's what Nest has created: a way for thermostats and other gadgets that regulate our environments to work within the context of our stories, not to be simply bound by the functionality of the device.

Hospitality

People who travel for leisure want more than a comfortable bed for the night—they want the feeling of having experienced something unique. Five-star-hotels that once felt like a luxury suddenly feel like a foolish, homogenous indulgence that lacks soul, something that anyone with deep enough pockets can buy. What many travellers want is to encounter places like a local, and hotels don't truly cater to that. Enter Airbnb, the company that unlocked the latent value in unused spaces by building a platform that didn't just sell a room for the night, but facilitated a connection between two people who had no way of knowing that they could trust each other.

Education

One of the problems of educating children *en masse* is the difficulty of accommodating varying levels of understanding and learning styles. Enter Khan Academy, which gives people the opportunity to learn at their own pace, to put the teacher on rewind, to shrink the gaps in their understanding and leap ahead if they need to—and to personalise their education, leaving behind the one-size-fits-all world of education and life.

KNOWING VS UNDERSTANDING

I hope there will be fewer attempts to try and show
'we know you' through the breadcrumbs of your data,
fewer business models based on selling access to people's
information and more attempts to do things for people,
not things that use people.
—GARETH KAY, CO-FOUNDER, CHAPTER

The UK supermarket giant Tesco was the darling of retail throughout the 1990s and into the new millennium, but in 2014, the company hit an eleven-year low, losing half of its market value. Let's look at how that happened.

Tesco became famous as a digital pioneer of the grocery industry. By tapping into customer buying behaviours with its Clubcard loyalty program (which launched in 1995), Tesco tracked what people did and then leveraged that knowledge to give people more of what Tesco wanted to sell them. As Michael Schrage points out in the *Harvard Business Review*, 'More than any other retailer of scale, Tesco had committed to customer research, analytics, and loyalty as its marketing and operational edge.' The Clubcard initiative, and the responsiveness that it enabled throughout the business, was said to be the catalyst that led to Tesco's 30 percent market share.

And Tesco rode the wave for two decades until something changed. While Tesco was busy watching what people did in their supermarkets, they forgot to notice that their customers' sentiment was shifting. Post-global-financial-crisis Tesco was busy giving out points for loyalty, when what customers wanted was the simplicity and transparency of cheaper prices across the board, without the gimmicks and incentives to buy the products the supermarket wanted to sell that week. As their circumstances and mindsets shifted, UK customers also began forsaking the big weekly shopping trips. Discount stores like Aldi and Lidl started to erode Tesco's market share as pounds in people's pockets became more meaningful than points collected on a loyalty card.

Clearly, watching what people do is not the same as paying attention to how they feel. The kind of hard data Tesco was collecting didn't tell the whole story in the context of the changing circumstances that people were managing. The data told Tesco what happened in the store, but that was just a tiny slice of what the customers were living. The data measured the customers' relationships to the business and the brand, but it couldn't accurately measure how they were feeling in the moment.

How we interpret both hard and soft data matters (smiles and frowns are data, too). Sometimes we use it to confirm our assumptions rather than to question them. Despite all they thought they knew, Tesco lost their market dominance by failing to stay relevant to people.

Loyalty cards can't replace genuine connection, and data analytics can't always measure what matters most. 'Meaningful' has to cut both ways.

MAKE THINGS PEOPLE WANT

There is nothing offensive, and there is nothing wrong or immoral, in people loving your brand for intangible, emotional reasons.
—Sir Martin Sorrell, CEO, WPP Group

In the world of mass marketing, doing business was about making things and then finding ways to make people want those things, and businesses created value by owning the means of production and building monopolies. Today, meaning and value are created at the intersection of the customer's worldview and your understanding of how your product aligns with that worldview.

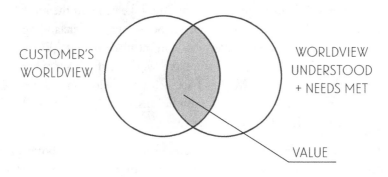

We know now that great products and services are born by obsessing about the user's feelings and frustrations—by understanding the problem to solve, for whom—and knowing the context in which people will use and benefit from those products and services. So, what are some of the ways we see this intersection of products and worldviews, in both the marketing of products and the creation of them?

In 2014, 716 million people visited IKEA's 360 stores. With annual sales just shy of $38 billion, IKEA is clearly a company that makes things that people want, but how does it duplicate its success across cultures? Well, if I told you that it took IKEA six years from the idea to the opening of the company's first store in South Korea, that would offer up some clues. Six years of research in order to understand the country's unique culture and the worldviews of the prospective customers they were building the store for so that they could tell a story that resonated.

There's a reason the IKEA catalogue comes in sixty-seven versions and thirty-two languages: the company knows that their products are worthless if they don't fit the context in which customers will use them. As the IKEA website says:

> 'At home' isn't just a place. It's a feeling. Like being in the most comfortable space in the universe. So for us, understanding people's life at home is the most natural place to start. Every year, we visit homes all around the world to find out what people dream about. We then pair their needs with the abilities of our suppliers to create new solutions that, hopefully, will make everyday life a little better.

This understanding that IKEA researchers seek affects both the development of products and their marketing. The Knapper, for example—a standing mirror that lets you hang clothes behind it—was designed to help people start their days more calmly by giving them a place to set out their clothes the night before. But IKEA's extensive research can influence product development only so much. Because IKEA's business model depends on volume, they can't change their products for different markets. It's essential, therefore, that the in-store room displays fit each country's culture. A bedroom in Japan might feature tatami mats and the earthquake beams that go through so many

Japanese flats, while an American bedroom might be larger and show a bed covered in pillows. In China, writes Eric Lin of Siegel+Gale, 'Room displays are presented to resemble the typical Chinese home, which places a strong emphasis on the living room … and less on bedrooms.'

Lin points out that store locations and services are also adapted to different cultures. Because car ownership is not common in China, IKEA stores are built in city centres. 'And in a region where "do-it-yourself" furniture concepts were practically unheard of prior to IKEA, the company offers far more delivery and assembly options than it does anywhere else in the world.'

People often say, 'Well, that's all very well for IKEA or (insert global brand name here) with their massive marketing and research and development budgets. How does any of this work for the little guy?' If you think about it, the little guy is often closer to his customers and has a greater opportunity to pay attention to what they want.

Take Flow Hive as an example. Stuart and Cedar Anderson, a father-and-son team of beekeepers turned inventors, knew firsthand the pain of harvesting honey from the hive. They spent ten years immersed in solving that problem, and three years developing a hive that would change the way honey was harvested. When they launched a crowdfunding campaign on Indiegogo, they raised over $12 million from more than 36,000 backers because beekeepers were lining up to buy a hive that was the answer to their prayers, allowing them to get honey from the hive without disturbing the bees. (For more information, see the Flow Hive case study later in this book.)

Innovation, sales and marketing are less about ideas and persuasion and more about understanding. We forget that. People don't want one more nudge in the direction we have decided they need to go. They need us to build our businesses around what we notice will make their lives better.

WHERE DID THOMAS EDISON START?

We will make electricity so cheap that only the rich will burn candles.
—THOMAS EDISON

It is well known that Thomas Edison didn't invent the light bulb, although he is often credited with it. Other inventors had been working for decades to solve the problem of finding a replacement for gaslight and creating a more efficient, safer lighting solution—in fact, twenty-three light bulbs were developed before Edison's. But Edison was the inventor who went on to make electric light bulbs a commercial success, patenting the first commercially viable incandescent light bulb in 1880. The secret to making this idea fly was to make it practical and affordable. It wasn't enough that it worked. It had to work for everyone.

Edison sought to understand how his light bulbs would fit into the whole electrical system and into people's lives. The value wasn't merely in the discovery; it was in making that discovery accessible so that it created a difference.

EMOTIONAL CAPITAL

When my dad was growing up during the 1950s, in a very large single-parent family, there was never enough food to go around. Eleven mouths to feed meant that he lived in times of scarcity. There were days when he and his brothers waited outside the bakery late in the day with hessian sacks ready to collect the stale bread that would be thrown out that evening. Within the family, anything that could be passed down was—threadbare coats and worn-out shoes were handed down and on and had several lives. What mattered was that they were functional and useful.

In those days, manufacturing standards varied, so quality was an advantage; it was something that a business owner could lead and differentiate with. Producing high-quality products that lasted meant that you could charge extra. Today most products are good enough. Standards are adequate across the board. Our frame for 'lasting' has changed. We don't expect to sit on the same sofas for twenty years like our parents and their parents did. We like our fashion fast; the faster it gets from catwalk to retailer, the better. We accept (sometimes reluctantly) that the life of a smartphone might be two years at best, while expecting an exceptional user experience as standard for any product or service.

So, what's left? We have come to care about all parts of the buying journey as much as we care about ownership. That mindset is reflected in how much we now value design and in how much time, thought, care and money companies devote to creating the perfect unboxing experience.

> Innovation today is inextricably linked with design—and design has become a decisive advantage in countless industries, not to mention a crucial tool to ward off commoditization.
> —*Cliff Kuang, Director of Product, Fast Company*

What design does—and not one of us who has seen the rise of companies like Apple, Beats and Nike can argue with this—is create value by building emotional capital. Today we expect products and services to be useful—and personalised and beautiful.

THE CONTEXT REVOLUTION

Sustainable businesses have long been built on understanding the importance of how people decide, as much as on knowing what they buy. And great innovations are born from believing that the way people use a product is just as important as how it works. In our 'age of abundance', it has never been more crucial for the innovator and marketer to pay attention to how the user or customer wants to experience a product or service. The way our consumption of content has evolved is the perfect example of that. More than half of digital content is consumed on a mobile device, and that fact has implications not just for the kind and quality of content we create, but also for the way it's presented to the audience we hope to reach.

What's true for content is true for anything we want people to invest in. We have less chance of engaging with our audience if we don't fully understand the context in which they will use our product, no matter how good that product is.

The desire for a more personalised experience has spawned multiple trends and innovations, as people strive to add meaning to their lives while removing friction. Companies like Disney have taken heed of those desires by creating ever more magical moments for their guests.

Disney's MagicBand is an all-in-one device that uses radio-frequency identification (RFID) technology to enable visitors to the theme park to have frictionless holidays. The MagicBand leverages data from sensors and users to create the ultimate in experiences that seemingly anticipate the visitor's every need. No need for tickets, cash, itineraries or menus as your MagicBand records your preselected choices and credit card details.

It's not just global brands that are pioneering these shifts. People in search of meaning are powering the success of platforms, products and services that matter to them and are spawning trends in product and service development as a result, proving that if we want to get inside people's wallets, we first need to get inside their heads and, more important, their hearts.

Let's look at some of these trends.

The Crowdfunded Economy

The Kickstarter generation has given rise to a new kind of patronage for the digital age. People can decide which projects matter to them and have skin in the game. They can say, 'this deserves to exist' and then be part of making that happen by pledging money to a creative project or a cause through a platform like Kiva.org, which allows people to pledge microloans to entrepreneurs in the developing world.

Social Capital, Curating and Upvoting

There is no doubt about the power of our social networks to influence our decisions and behaviours. It's been proven that people are more likely to buy things based on the recommendation of a friend. In fact, 71 percent of us are more likely to make purchases based on social media referrals. Our likes, tweets, upvotes, reviews and recommendations on all kinds of digital platforms, like Yelp, Product Hunt and Airbnb, have the power to change the perception of a product or service.

Personalisation

We expect our experiences to be tailored to our needs and lifestyles. A report from TrendWatching.com identifies the ability to personalise everything as one aspect of what it calls 'post-demographic consumerism':

Individuals are able to personalize—and express themselves through—their consumption to a greater degree than ever before.

This is being driven at a macro level by the global expansion of the consumer class and the explosion of product choice in mature markets. But it's being driven at the level of the individual, too, with digital experimentation allowing for a greater range of experiences at lower cost, and online social networks (enthusiastically used by all demographics) allowing people to identify with brands, products and services—even those that they don't or can't purchase.

It's no accident that you can customise your new Apple Watch with one of thirty-eight bands or that it comes in different sizes, because people's wrists do, too. Alan Dye, the head of Apple's human interface group, studied the watch industry and learned that 'personalization and beauty are everything, and the only way to get one company's product onto different people's wrists is to offer options—sizes, materials, bands—for a wide range of tastes and budgets.'

We can't help but be drawn in by emails that address us by name or services that allow us to express our individuality. Companies are getting wise to the fact that we want to customise everything from our coffee (there are over 80,000 possible combinations at Starbucks) to our shoes (fifteen shades of grey at Shoes of Prey). And so businesses where we can create beautiful, personalised photo books, like Artifact Uprising, or bespoke perfume studios where we can design our own unique fragrances are growing and thriving.

It seems that the more ways brands can give us to feel we are one of a kind, the better.

The Internet of Things

The darlings of the context revolution are products and services like the Nest self-learning thermostat and the Waze real-time traffic-information application, which capture data and use it to help save us time and money (and even avoid speeding tickets by alerting us to hidden police patrols). Despite concerns about privacy, we are reasonably happy to trade some privacy for convenience and trade data for more meaningful experiences. (Privacy concerns vary among demographics; millennials, for example, are less concerned about digital privacy than other generations are.)

Subscription Services and Tailored Recommendations

Services that thoughtfully add value by saving people time, money and head space are springing up across all sectors. Everything from groceries to tampons, inspirational posters to nappies, entertainment to cosmetics can be bought via subscription.

The other way these service providers create value is by using our data to recommend other related products, services and entertainment we might enjoy. Book and TV show recommendations from Amazon or Netflix, based on our tastes, actually feel helpful and change marketing from push to pull.

Values-Based Purchasing Decisions

Brands like Method and Warby Parker that have become B corporations—'certified by the non-profit B Lab to meet rigorous standards of social and environmental performance, accountability, and transparency'—recognise the benefits of transparency and the intangible value to their customers of being businesses that operate for good. Increasingly people want to do business with brands whose business practices reflect their personal values.

Tribal Brands

From Crossfit to Coffee Geeks, Harley owners to Sharkies, belonging is not just a badge of honour; it's part of the story we tell ourselves about who we are, and one of the reasons we pay a premium for brands that become part of that narrative.

The Quest for Significance

Self-improvement, both physical and psychological, is a multibillion-dollar industry. Technology now helps us to measure and track and compare our personal performance. Fitness trackers, monitors and apps give us ways to monitor our progress and, in theory, help us to work towards our goals.

Startup Culture

Taking advantage of the reach that technology gives them, more people are choosing to become freelancers, entrepreneurs and independent creatives who are in charge of their own destinies. Interestingly, a slew of online platforms and tools have been spawned on the back of this shift. Upwork, Kickstarter, QuickBooks and on and on are all meeting the needs of a new breed of entrepreneurs and indie artists.

On-Demand Everything

The technological revolution hasn't just given us more access to information; it's opened the door for companies and organisations to offer increasingly relevant and more customer-centric logistics services. Gone are the days when you had no choice but to wrestle with car keys, children and traffic to line up at the grocery store or take-away restaurant. Services like Postmates and Instacart connect customers with local couriers, who buy and deliver groceries and other goods to your door within an hour.

Shift from Legacy Brands

Increasingly we buy from companies that reflect the stories we believe about who we are, brands that support the narrative of our lives and values. Fledgling brands like The Honest Company—founded by Jessica Alba and Christopher Gavigan to introduce safe, eco-friendly nappies and other baby products to the market—can find a place in the hearts of consumers, not by going head-to-head with legacy brands like Procter & Gamble, but by doing things that legacy brands find harder to do because of their size, complexity and organisational structure. It's not easy to turn around a big ship that's answerable to shareholders and instead focus on things customers care about, like social responsibility, transparency, sustainability and the intangible value of knowing you are buying something that will do as little harm as possible to the people you care about and to the world you want your children and grandchildren to grow up in.

The Reputation Economy

A brand's reputation is everything and trust creates value. In the old days, trust was budgeted for and bought by shelf space and broadcast on advertising billboards. Today, platforms like TaskRabbit and Airbnb enable one-man-bands and part-time service providers to create value that is built around a currency of trust.

Artisanal, Local

Etsy, the online platform founded in 2005 to let craftsmen and -women sell their wares directly to customers, now hosts shops for 1.5 million artisans and is valued at $1.5 billion, proof that the maker movement is alive and well. There are enough people who care about the origins of and stories behind the things they buy to want to pay a bit more than they would for the homogenous products sold at big-box stores.

A similar shift is happening in the food industry. Local and regional food sales in the U.S. grew from US$4.8 billion in 2008 to US$6.1 billion in 2012. Many people want to connect with the people who grew their food and want to know how many miles it travelled to reach their plates.

WHO IS RESPONSIBLE FOR SEEING YOUR CUSTOMERS?

And if you have an area you're working, talk to customers. Every day. Talk to users of your product, active, inactive, new, and old. Talk to people who don't want to use your product. Talk to people who are using a competitor's product. Talk to customers of products in adjacent markets. Now, reread this paragraph and replace talk with listen. Understand how customers see the world. They don't know the solutions, but they know the problems well. If you haven't talked to a customer today, you're doing it wrong.

The simple fact is that the majority of great software startups today ... required no technical insight to start, and you can always hire experts to help you scale. The driver of these innovations is an uncommon understanding of what the customer (aka humans) wants or how to deliver an understood solution in a better way.
—STARTUP L. JACKSON

It's easier than ever to get an opinion from your customers or potential customers. A simple 140-character tweet will yield a slew of opinions about what you're building or what people might want or buy. Focus groups have been relied on for decades to help businesses and brands find out what people say they prefer in the moment, but focus groups don't make allowances for human nature, which often leads us to say things we don't mean and mean things we don't say.

Seeing your customers isn't simply about sending out lists of questions in a survey or getting confirmation that your idea is a good one. It's about investing time, energy and resources to understand their lives, their challenges, hopes, dreams and fears, to figure out how whatever you're creating has a chance of addressing some of those.

Dylan Blanchard is a UX researcher at Shopify, the platform that has enabled more than 150,000 entrepreneurs and counting to sell their products online ($3.7 billion worth in 2014) and to shape the kind of experiences they offer to their customers. In an article on Medium.com, he wrote about the importance of listening to and learning from the shop owners:

> Every day I'm lucky enough to talk to shop owners that run their businesses on Shopify. These are some of the most brilliant entrepreneurs, pairing amazing products with perfect execution.
>
> Each time I sit down to chat with one of them, we discuss how their business is doing, what's happening in their world, and what's on the horizon—we talk shop (both figuratively and literally) ... It's the golden opportunity for me as a researcher to address [their uncertainty] head on and remind this entrepreneur of the whole reason we're chatting—to appreciate what they do, to understand how they do it, and most simply, to just learn from them.
>
> —*Dylan Blanchard*

What I love about Dylan's story and the Shopify customer development story is that Shopify doesn't create anything (however elegant a solution it seems) without understanding how it's going to help a person to run her business in the real world. If it isn't going to benefit 80 percent of their customers 80 percent of the time, then it probably isn't going to get built. That's no mean feat when your customers are as big as Google and as tiny as a stay-at-home mum operating a kitchen-table business, but knowing where their customers started and where they hope to go makes all the difference.

part 3

THE OPPORTUNITY WITHIN REACH

If everyone is busy making everything, how can anyone perfect anything? We start to confuse convenience with joy. Abundance with choice. Digital infinity. Designing something requires focus. The first thing we ask is: What do we want people to feel? Delight. Surprise. Love. Connection. Then we begin to craft around our intention. It takes time. There are a thousand no's for every yes. We simplify, we perfect, we start over, until everything we touch enhances each life it touches.
—Apple 'Intention' video

THE NEW RULES OF BRAND AWARENESS

Many prospective clients come to me asking for help to tell their story so that they can attract customers and create brand awareness.

For decades, businesses have created brand awareness by following four rules—which no longer work.

Old rules of brand awareness:

1. Make something for everyone.
2. Tell our story.
3. Attract customers.
4. Build brand awareness.

The brands that succeed today have flipped things around.

New rules of brand awareness:

1. Understand the customers' story.
2. Make something they want.
3. Give them a story to tell.
4. Create brand affinity.

While we are scurrying around employing this tactic and that one in order to get more people to notice us, we are overlooking the greatest opportunity we have to drive the growth and success of our businesses.

Awareness of our products and services is not what spreads our stories.

Our stories spread when we are aware of our customers.

FUNCTIONALITY, FEATURES OR FEELINGS?

As business owners, innovators, creatives and leaders, we often attempt to divorce business from life as if we and our customers suddenly have a different modus operandi when it comes to buying or selling. Real estate sales copy is a classic example of this. Wherever I have lived, the copy on brochures of homes for sale seems to serve one purpose—to fill the space between the images and the floor plan in the brochure. There is a lot of talk about abodes and allotments and not enough of a story about the cool summer breezes and cosy winter afternoons in front of the fire. People are being asked to make significant financial decisions based only on the facts, when everyone knows that we buy with our hearts first and our heads later.

That's why fashion brand Kit and Ace don't describe their products; they tell the story of the customer's life with those products in it. An $88 scarf isn't a scarf; it's a 'cashmere hug on a cold day. Like the first sip of soup on a cold day or a warm body curled up beside you under the blankets, surrounding yourself in warmth tops the list of simple pleasures.'

You might think that this is just a clever marketing ploy—a sales trick employed in order to sell more stuff, but if the story shows the customer that you've seen her and makes her purchase more meaningful, is that manipulation or is it a gift?

The bottom line is that people don't just buy the thing, they buy the feeling, so knowing what feelings your products and services are designed to elicit is just as important as knowing what features to leave out or put in.

GIVING A DAMN AND THE TRIPLE BOTTOM LINE

He profits most who serves best.
—ARTHUR F. SHELDON

It's no longer enough to operate a business simply to profit, without caring about how that business affects both the people it serves and the world in which it operates. A selfish, single bottom line simply won't cut it anymore.

It's been twenty-one years since John Elkington coined the term 'triple bottom line' in 1994 to describe an accounting framework that asks businesses and organisations to evaluate success beyond simply measuring how much money they make and to include people, planet and profit in the equation. Increasingly our customers want to know that they are supporting businesses that care. They want to feel like their ideals and needs were considered, not merely leveraged to make money.

Companies that succeed in the eyes of the customers are the ones that think beyond financial results. When we care, people know, and brands that invest in creating meaning, alongside profitable businesses, are building remarkably successful businesses.

The Honest Company, founded in 2011 and now valued at a billion dollars, is an ethical consumer-goods company that manufactures and sells non-toxic baby and household products. The company uses organic and sustainable materials from renewable sources, a percentage of the sale of each product is donated to non-profits and the company has introduced a human-rights and environmental code of conduct for their suppliers.

THE CUSTOMER IS YOUR COMPASS

Code is easy, people are hard. It often takes the best engineers the longest to realize this.
—Startup L. Jackson

Before self-service shopping, online stores, social networks and recommendation platforms, the consumer's role was limited to buying what was on offer. Customers' purchases were dictated by availability and trends, their choices heavily influenced by advertising and seasonal availability and restricted by weekly budgets. It was a safe bet to conclude that if you got people through the door, you'd convert them to sales.

Today, in an era when shops have become showrooms and choice is real, not simply a marketing illusion, our customers are more than just passive consumers of our products and services. They are partners, co-creators, patrons, advocates, evangelists, collaborators and community members. People no longer just want to buy things from us without thinking—they want to become invested in the businesses and brands that they choose to support, and they want those brands to be a part of the stories they tell both to and about themselves.

This is a shift we can and should nurture, not to mention an opportunity we can leverage, not simply to sell more stuff but to do meaningful work that connects deeply with our customers.

The clothing manufacturer Patagonia employs forty-five full-time technicians who complete about 30,000 repairs per year. In the spring of 2015, the company set off on a coast-to-coast road trip across the U.S. in a biodiesel truck to repair their customers' 'tired and well-loved' clothing. Patagonia cares about fixing a jacket that has travelled the world with a customer because that act aligns with their company values, and just as important, it helps to deepen the bond between customer and company. Often the people who send garments in for repair also send their stories about how that piece of clothing has been with them through thick and thin. The customers' stories fuel Patagonia's story and have done so for over four successful decades.

The team at Patagonia believe that 'one of the most responsible things we can do as a company is to make high-quality stuff that lasts for years and can be repaired, so you don't have to buy more of it.' They innovate for and market to those customers who believe what they believe. The customer is their compass.

INVISIBLE PROBLEMS

*[I]t's seeing the invisible problem, not just the obvious
problem, that's important, not just for product design,
but for everything we do. You see, there are invisible
problems all around us, ones we can solve. But first we
need to see them, to feel them.*
—Tony Faddell, CEO, Nest

Like most women of her generation who visited New York in 1902, thirty-six-year-old Mary Anderson got to where she was going in a streetcar. On one particular wintery day, she couldn't help but notice how all hell broke loose on the city roads as soon as the weather turned nasty. When it began to rain or snow, every driver was in a mad panic to clear his window in order to see where he was going.

Today we take windscreen wipers for granted, and perhaps, like me, you imagined that they were invented along with the car. Not so. When bad weather struck, the driver had to roll down the window and stick his head out the side of the car in an attempt to see the road and oncoming traffic. He sometimes used his hand to clear the windscreen, but that wasn't very effective. The lucky ones might have had a split windshield, half of which could be opened to let the driver see out, but that wasn't very useful or practical and it didn't improve visibility and safety all that much.

This situation inspired Mary to think about creating a solution to the problem, which would only get worse as more cars came on the roads. When she returned home to Alabama, Mary worked with a designer to create the first manually operated windscreen wiper, which she obtained the patent for in 1903 (it expired in 1920). It would take almost two more decades for wipers to become standard on new automobiles.

What Mary hit on a century ago was the solution to what Tony Fadell—the creator of the iPod and CEO of Nest—calls an 'invisible problem'. That's a problem that we don't think of as being a problem because we're so used to it, we just don't see it anymore and don't think about ways that things could be different or better.

The businesses that have been runaway successes over the past three decades are the ones that have taken the time to find out what their customers are feeling. That's what has enabled them to design meaningful products and services. The Zappos, Apples, Nests, Shopifys and Patagonias of this world make someone responsible for seeing, not just serving, their customers.

Shopify logged over 30,000 hours of call time in 2014. That's a lot of time spent listening to what your customers are experiencing in order to interpret what they want.

The design and human interface teams at Apple spent two years thinking about what a wrist-mounted device could add to peoples' lives—all the while questioning how they could make our need for digital connectedness less intrusive and more human. The resulting hardware and software were developed by understanding how we would use it—not just to make it work. It turns out that insanely great functionality is useless without a user experience to match. And so the Apple Watch prioritises information according to the wearer's reaction to it. For example, after notifying the user that a text message has been received, the 'Short Look' feature either displays the message or leaves it unread, depending on how long the user keeps her wrist aloft. The ability of the software to interpret signals from the user is what makes the product more meaningful than another device. So does the hardware's ability to notify you with taps and sounds that are just enough to do the job and not so distracting that you'll want to take the watch off.

You don't need the resources of a Fortune 500 company or a human interface design team to develop an understanding of your customers. What you do need is to recognise the importance of doing that as the first step to creating products and services that matter to the people who use them.

HARD DATA AND SOFT DATA

[N]umbers, however rubbish they are, have the appearance of objectivity ... Creativity is very heavily policed, but shallow rationality is allowed to run rampant.
—RORY SUTHERLAND, VICE-CHAIRMAN, OGILVY GROUP UK

It seems like a no-brainer to suppose that local businesses like cafés, dry cleaners or doctor's surgeries—the kinds of businesses that serve the same customers regularly, where the staff have the opportunity to look their customers in the eye—would take advantage of the fact that they look their customers in the eye.

Bricks-and-mortar businesses have the advantage of intimacy, unlike online businesses, which must collect a ton of (often valuable) hard data to learn more about their customers and determine how to give them what they want. Digital businesses need to use hard data in an attempt to replicate intimacy. But the waiter sees the wrinkled nose, the barista remembers the regular and the doctor hears the stories that inputs from the keyboard can never fully communicate.

There is a lot of talk about how responsive organisations are winning in today's new economy, a world where people expect levels of service, personalisation and relevance that were devalued and lost to them in a top-down industrial economy. We hear about the winners who are positioned to take all, the Googles and the Amazons, digital behemoths who are leveraging hard data to create platforms that connect us to our wants and to each other. And yet, the opportunity to create value from the soft data we collect every day, in the form of feedback, stories and gestures from loyal customers, remains largely untapped in a world that's focused on taking advantage of hard data.

The job of every single business on the planet is to do just one thing—to make people happy. When you find ways to do that, you win.

Once our basic needs are taken care of, the thing that we want most as humans is to matter.

As the structure and social fabric of our towns and cities change, there is a huge opportunity for local businesses to fill some of the void that a lack of belonging to a community has created. Velo Cult, a bicycle shop cum community hub in Portland, Oregon, has a coffee bar and a museum and it hosts events almost every day. This is one example of how businesses can become more than just providers of goods and services and in some cases become part of the fabric of their customers' lives.

Instead of simply trying to get the order processed or the sale over the line, we could be looking for opportunities to connect with how people feel and to understand what matters to them.

Before online retailer Black Milk Clothing releases a new collection, they preview the new lines on Pinterest. The number of comments and likes for each image helps them predict which styles will be popular, so they can adjust production levels accordingly.

Making sense of the information our customers give us, both consciously and unconsciously—and then doing something that creates value with what we make of that data—is where the opportunity to create meaning lies. What could be more valuable to our businesses than taking what we know about people and using it to improve how we serve them?

FRICTIONLESS

Increasingly what we value are products and services that remove friction from our lives. We want to prioritise the important and delegate and outsource the things we don't find meaningful, so we can leave time for the things that really matter to us. Our new world doesn't allow time for boredom, unproductive days or fruitless effort—it's a world in which no second is wasted. Waiting has become a thing of the past and queuing an option; like many things, it's become something that we are willing to pay to avoid. Time is the new money and do-it-for-me services are flourishing. We can now outsource everything from our DIY to our book reading, from dinner to admin.

The leveraging of technology in every area of our lives is conditioning us to expect increasing levels of relevance. Our online activity gives businesses and brands the opportunity to engage with us in ways that are more subtle and less obtrusive than a banner ad or a billboard. In our new digital world, we expect our needs to be anticipated and for things to happen automagically. Those expectations are being carried over into the analogue world. Our expectations of and relationships with the companies we buy from will continue to shift as the products we buy become more than utilitarian objects or one-off purchases. Connected devices extend the obligation of the innovator from providing a product that works, and likely never hearing from the customer again unless the product fails within the warranty period, to being in an ongoing trusting relationship with the customer as data is gathered and software is updated. Subscription services shift the buyer-and-seller relationship from transactional to sustained and continuous.

An on-demand economy of products and services, like Instacart, Shyp, Uber and Caviar—enabled by mobile devices, sensors and humans—is changing our perceptions and creating a new normal in the service industry. We now expect to book restaurant reservations, theatre tickets, and travel arrangements online, and if we live in large cities, we expect to get grocery or other deliveries within an hour or two. I bet you scratched your head the last time you walked past an empty high-street travel agency.

If we can find ways to buy back meaning (even at a premium), we will. And sometimes the way we buy back meaning is to buy convenience so we can spend our precious time on the activities that matter to us.

Tony Fadell, CEO of Nest, tells a great story about how they wanted to make the installation of the Nest thermostat as easy as possible for new users. When Nest first launched, they shipped three kinds of screws so the thermostat could be installed on different surfaces. Soon after shipping, the team realised that users were not having a great experience, so they went back to the drawing board, as Fadell says, 'much to the chagrin of our investors', who asked, 'Why are you spending so much time on a little screw? Get out there and sell more!' The team's response? 'We will sell more if we get this right.' They did. Nest Labs was acquired by Google in 2014 for $3.2 billion, just three and a half years after the company was founded.

Which means that Nest isn't alone in needing to get this right.

CHARACTERISTICS OF DISRUPTIVE INNOVATIONS

Disruptive innovations:

1. Start with a purpose and a small problem, rather than a big idea.
2. Are based on what people do, not what they say they do.
3. Leverage data to get closer to users, customers or fans.
4. Can be more responsive to customers' behaviours and needs.
5. Tap into consumers' latent desires.
6. Connect the disconnected.
7. Create value where none existed.
8. Disrupt people's lives, not industries—aligning with the user's worldview and often changing what people believe is possible for them, thus changing their behaviour.
9. Begin by facilitating or creating change for a small group of people at the edges.
10. Seem obvious only after the fact.

THE POWER OF NOTICING

Making things is an art. Making things meaningful is an art and a science.

When we understand what doesn't work, we can fix it.

When we know what people want, we can give it to them.

When we realise what people care about, we can create more meaningful experiences.

When we make things people love, we don't have to make people love our things.

When our values align with the worldviews of our customers, we succeed.

When business exists to create meaning, not just money, we all win.

part 4

THE STORY STRATEGY BLUEPRINT

*The successful strategists of the future will have a
holistic, empathetic understanding of customers and
be able to convert somewhat murky insights into a
creative business model that they can prototype
and revise in real time.*
—ROGER MARTIN, AUTHOR

WHO IS YOUR MUSE?

At the start of her nationwide tour in 1974, the famous actress and singer Connie Francis returned to her motel room in Long Island, where she was brutally attacked at knifepoint. The tragic story made headlines around the world. Tor Sørnes, a lock engineer from Norway, was so distressed on hearing the reports that he started working on a system that would provide a unique key for every hotel guest. Tor immediately understood that it was time to do something about the system that had existed for generations—one that no longer met the customers' need to feel safe and secure. He went on to pioneer the invention of the recodable keycard lock.

For a high school principal with a background of educating children in some of the toughest schools in Philadelphia, the single most important resource in Linda Cliatt-Wayman's arsenal as she strives to improve standards and create meaningful change is a real understanding of her students. As she explains in her recent TED Talk,

> So, if I'm going to push my students toward their dream and their purpose in life, I've got to get to know who they are. So I have to spend time with them, so I manage the lunchroom every day. And while I'm there, I talk to them about deeply personal things, and when it's their birthday, I sing 'Happy Birthday' even though I cannot sing at all. I often ask them, 'Why do you want me to sing when I cannot sing at all?' And they respond by saying, 'Because we like feeling special.'

> We hold monthly town hall meetings to listen to their concerns, to find out what is on their minds. They ask us questions like, 'Why do we have to follow rules?' 'Why are there so many consequences?' 'Why can't we just do what we want to do?' They ask, and I answer each question honestly, and this exchange in listening helps to clear up any misconceptions.

German shoemaker and keen sportsman Adolf (Adi) Dassler became obsessed with watching athletes in order to understand how the equipment they used could make them better. He realised that because each athlete had a unique set of abilities and techniques, he also needed unique footwear to perform his best. In 1936, Adi handmade a pair of running shoes for one of the most successful track and field athletes of all time, Jesse Owens, who went on to win four gold medals. Adi designed the first screw-in studded football boots, which were famed for leading the German team to a second-half victory in the wet and slippery conditions of the 1954 World Cup final. He created two different shoes adapted to the technique of Olympic gold medallist high-jumper Dick Fosbury (who invented the revolutionary, now universally used Fosbury Flop).

Like Tor, Linda and Adi, every great innovator or change maker has a muse who is the catalyst that ignites their vision of what could be— someone whose life will be different and better when she lives in a world with their product or service in it.

If we are to create something meaningful (that includes a product, service or environment that changes people), we must think beyond stereotypes and buyer personas that provide us with fictional, generalised representations based on our assumptions of our ideal customers and audiences. Our competitors are already using and exploiting those personas to death anyway! We need inspiration beyond descriptors that compartmentalise and reduce people to age, gender, education, income, lifestyle, buying habits and decision-making stereotypes. We have to really see the world through their eyes and observe them experiencing it in real time (not just in a focus group complete with loaded questions) in order to understand how anything we create can make a difference.

In a recent presentation, Fred Dust, a partner at IDEO, said something that made my heart sing: 'You're a better designer if you love the people you're designing for.'

This is not easy for a respected professional to say in any business setting (what a shame), and even Fred, who has an extraordinary track record in innovation and human-centred design, felt awkward about saying it. He was almost apologetic to the people in the audience, some of whom he knew would find this a hard thing to swallow. 'Love' is not a word we are comfortable with using in business circles. Business by definition is transactional, not emotional. But what Fred hit on here is the one thing we need to hear (and live) most in business and not just in life. When you genuinely care about and empathise with the people you make things for, those things can't help but become meaningful.

It turns out that the best way to create a solution is to name someone's problem or aspiration. Meaningful solutions are those that are created for actual people with problems, limitations, frustrations, wants, needs, hopes, dreams and desires that we then have a chance of fulfilling. These solutions are born from investing time in hearing what people say, watching what they do (or don't do, but want to) and caring about them enough to want to solve that problem or create that solution that takes them to where they want to go.

WORLDVIEWS

A worldview is a point of view, a way of seeing the world. Worldviews are not formed objectively and supported by facts. They are subjective, values-based reflections of our experiences and beliefs.

Our worldviews shape our attitudes and biases, influence our decisions and guide our actions. And while as innovators and marketers we understand all of this, in our search for ways to understand and define our markets, we sometimes forget to apply it.

Just because they take the same route to work each morning doesn't mean that all twenty-nine-year-old men living in the suburbs share the same worldview. Our assumptions about the stories of the people we create for can lead us down the wrong track.

One of my astute readers, Tim Graham of Integrity Fitness, captures the importance of understanding worldviews like this:

I have older people coming to fitness classes with young people's music, loud stuff like dubstep. Most fitness offerings would place them in a category of 'older adults' and give them something they assume they want or need. But maybe they'd like to feel young again? Exercise does that, but maybe a 'young' environment works better for them. Maybe they don't want 'old folks' exercise?

If what people believe influences their choices just as much as, if not more than, how much they have to spend, then we need to focus our attention on their hearts and not just their wallets.

WHERE CAN YOU TAKE THE CUSTOMER?

Think of your product or service as the catalyst or enabler of something in the life of customers and users. Describe their lives before your product (café, software, app, yoga pants) became part of their stories and then their lives after it.

These before and after scenarios are important because they allow you to articulate the change that happens because your product exists. When you understand how the customer's story will unfold in the presence of your product and how that product helps to shape his new reality, then you can work backwards to the feelings that the features and functionality must create in order to move your customer from here to there.

Any one of a number of giant companies could have been first to market with a bagless vacuum cleaner. They all knew that their cleaners lost suction when dust bags became full. They also knew how their customers wrestled to empty dust bags while being enveloped by the dirt they'd just sucked out of their carpets. Taxi companies were aware that people found waiting for cabs frustrating, and watching the meter running while they were stuck in a traffic jam unnerving. Big hotel chains understood that their guests wanted more personal service and resented the inflated prices charged for items from the minibar.

And yet it took smaller players like Dyson, Uber and Airbnb to respond to those needs and bring about change: an easier way to keep floors clean; peace of mind for taxi passengers; a friendlier (and less expensive) place to stay while travelling. So how and why were these companies able to succeed in disrupting a market?

Disruptive innovators thrive on creating difference first and focus on growth later. As I said earlier, they almost never begin by designing a product—they always start by understanding the problem to be solved, and that problem always belongs to someone specific, who has a particular worldview. Just as the exchange of stories is as much about listening as it is about telling, innovation is as much about understanding as it is about creating.

THE INNOVATION TRIFECTA

Take a moment to think about the most successful products and services of our time. I don't even have to name them—you know what they are and the tiny handful of companies that invented them. Now consider why these products succeeded where others failed. Their form and functionality—how they looked and worked—were non-negotiables, but it's the way they made people feel when they used and experienced them that set them apart.

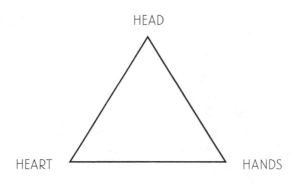

It turns out that there is no way to divorce the demands of the head and the needs of the hands from the longing of the heart.

START WITH THEIR STORY

If we can agree that your market is defined by someone's need, not by your idea, then we can also agree that in order to create an idea that flies, you must start with the potential customer's story. But—oh boy—that is so much easier to say than it is to do!

We can't help falling in love with our ideas, being influenced by our biases and acting on our assumptions; that very fact is the reason so many fail. It's hard to be rational or objective about something you've poured your heart and soul into—the thing that you are invested in having succeed, no matter what the odds. It's not easy for an organisation to kill a goose that is laying a golden egg today in order to make a bigger bet on what the future will look like (Kodak and Blackberry being just two examples of that). This is something I witness every day as I work with entrepreneurs and companies to help them find opportunities to grow their businesses by allowing customers to play a bigger part in their brand stories.

The tool that I'm about to share with you started life as part of a brand-storytelling-strategy project I worked on with the innovation department of a Fortune 500 company. We were charged with finding a way for the team to get closer to experiencing the world as their product's user would. We needed to help them to empathise with the user and see the world as he did. The team wanted something to remind them to focus first on the end user before settling themselves in front of their CAD programs when the user wasn't right in front of them. The tool was designed to force team members to get out from behind their desks and do what the greatest innovators and marketers of our time have done—go experience what the customer is experiencing. The blueprint I created for them wasn't as refined as this one has become in the months that followed and as I wrote this book to explain it to you, but it did serve the purpose of beginning the innovation journey by understanding the customer's perspective.

The blueprint started with their story, and it starts with yours, too—with your desire to create ideas that fly.

THE LEVEL OF LOVE

When a company cares about its staff, suppliers, customers and the way it shows up in and affects the world, that caring is reflected in the products and services the company creates. It's easy to spot thoughtful design or to taste the difference between hand churned and factory made. And yet we don't always give enough consideration to how the level of love we put into the products we make can differentiate the work that we do and become a competitive advantage.

Evidenced by the success of brands like Chipotle, Warby Parker, The Honest Company, Harry's, Death to the Stock Photo, Holstee, Johanna Basford, CreativeMornings, Flow Hive, Airbnb, Padre Coffee, Bahen & Co. and The Distillery (and I could keep going), I'm here to tell you once and for all that giving a damn is seriously underrated and caring is a competitive advantage. I believe that love can become a more significant differentiator only in a world where people increasingly care about purpose, individuality, sustainability, provenance and ethics. How we make is equally important as what we make. While there may not yet be room for the 'L' word in every boardroom, my hope is that you'll see the sense of making room for it in your business.

THE STORY STRATEGY BLUEPRINT

MAKE SOMETHING + MAKE PEOPLE LOVE IT
OR
LOVE PEOPLE + MAKE SOMETHING THEY LOVE

This equation is not new to readers of my blog. It's designed to explain as succinctly as possible why we're using our customer's story as the jumping-off point for developing products and services. This blueprint is designed to help you home in on the customer's worldview before you start out on your innovation journey. You can use the blueprint to create products, services, events, platforms and more, either as an individual or as part of a team. Whether you're designing a shoe or writing a blog post, the Story Strategy Blueprint will help you to create something that is more meaningful to your customers—something that satisfies their heads, works in their hands and speaks to their hearts—because it puts the audience at the centre.

As business owners and team leaders, we view our businesses through various lenses. We have a financial lens, a success lens, a marketing lens, a service lens and on and on depending on how complex our organisation is. We measure our performance in a hundred different ways, often neglecting the most significant metric of all—customer-worthiness. This is the most important lens we can apply, the most accurate measurement of meaningful work.

When everything you do is framed by the question 'Is this product or service worthy of my customer and why?' it changes everything.

Thus, the innovation journey on the Story Strategy Blueprint begins at point 1, with the prospective customer's story, and guides you through an exploration process that will help you translate her problems from opportunities to insights, and from insights to products and services that provide her with the features and benefits she needs and the emotional benefits she wants.

In the section following the blueprint, you will find case studies that illustrate how businesses big and small have followed a path along their innovation journeys similar to the one I hope the Story Strategy Blueprint puts you on.

THE STORY STRATEGY BLUEPRINT

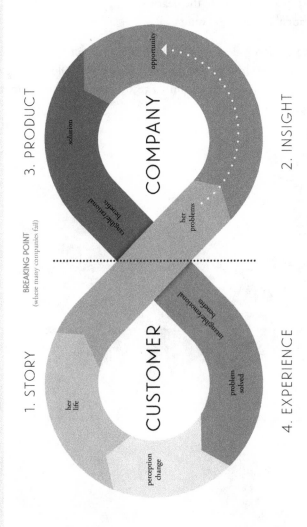

1. STORY

3. PRODUCT

2. INSIGHT

4. EXPERIENCE

BREAKING POINT
(where many companies fail)

COMPANY

CUSTOMER

opportunity

solution

tangible/rational benefits

her problems

intangible/emotional benefits

her life

perception change

problem solved

CASE STUDIES

Figure out what matters and build something good.
—EVAN WILLIAMS, CEO OF MEDIUM

The following case studies illustrate how the blueprint can be used. They are for illustration purposes only and are not intended to imply any endorsement by the companies profiled here.

To see them in larger format please visit meaningfulbook.com.

For guidance on applying the blueprint to your own work, please see 'Using the Story Strategy Blueprint', near the end of this book.

THE STORY STRATEGY BLUEPRINT

Created for ___Shoes of Prey___   Date ___April 19, 2015___

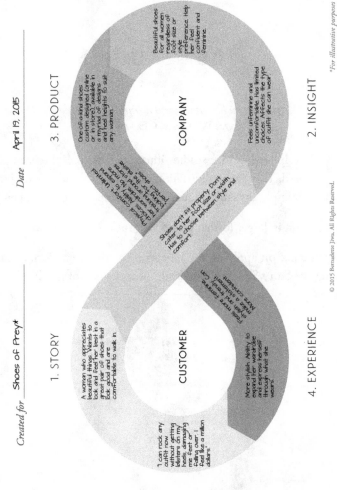

3. PRODUCT

COMPANY

Beautiful shoes for all women regardless of foot size or style preference. Help her feel confident and feminine.

One-of-a-kind shoes custom designed (online or in store), available in a myriad of designs and heel heights to suit any woman.

Physical comfort + Unlimited choice. No other shoes provide this blend of comfort and choice.

Shoes don't fit properly. Don't cater to her foot size or width. Has to choose between style and comfort.

Feels uniformed and uncomfortable. Has limited choice. Affects the type of outfit she can wear.

2. INSIGHT

1. STORY

CUSTOMER

A woman who appreciates beautiful things. Wants to look and feel her best in a great pair of shoes that look good and are comfortable to walk in.

"I can rock any outfit now without getting blisters on my heels, damaging me feet or feeling like a million dollars."

More stylish. Ability to expand her wardrobe and express herself through what she wears.

Feels more feminine. Can make a statement. More confident.

4. EXPERIENCE

*For illustrative purposes

SHOES OF PREY

Although she had invested years of her life studying law, Jodie Fox knew that her heart wasn't in a legal career, and she eventually found a way to tap into her creativity by working in advertising. Having a Sicilian mother, Jodie had always been surrounded by stylish clothes and beautiful shoes when she was growing up. But when she was finally earning enough to buy them, she could never find shoes that she liked. She resorted to getting a few bespoke pairs of shoes that she had designed made for her. The results were fabulous.

Whenever she wore her fabulous shoes, Jodie's friends commented on them, and when they discovered that she'd designed them, they inevitably asked if she could commission their shoe designs. The conversations that followed recounted their frustrating shoe-buying experiences. Jodie heard stories about not being able to find anything special and, perhaps worse, about spending a lot of money on shoes that didn't fit properly—shoes that were destined to remain in boxes at the back of wardrobes after a single uncomfortable evening of wear.

When she began to dig deeper, Jodie discovered that many women found it impossible to get shoes to fit them at all. If they were outside the standard Australian sizes of 5 to 10, there was little hope of finding anything. Some women told her stories about joyless shopping trips where they walked straight up to assistants and simply asked if they had even one pair of shoes in the store to fit them. Women with larger feet felt unfeminine, and those on either end of the 'normal' scale felt like they were missing out.

The reality is that how shoes are retailed affects how they are designed and manufactured. Shoes are typically mass-produced in batches in four or five styles, with heel heights and colours limited by the current season's trends. With so few options, women often have to choose between comfort and style.

By listening to potential customers, Jodie knew that there was a market for bespoke shoes that didn't fit the current business model or method of manufacture, but she recognised that she couldn't deliver what those women wanted without enlisting the help of some savvy business partners. Jodie teamed up with Mike Knapp and Michael Fox (ex-Google employees with backgrounds in engineering and online retail), and the three began to investigate the possibility of starting a business that would make custom shoes, one pair at a time.

And so Shoes of Prey was born—launched in 2009, the company makes shoes in thirty-eight shoe sizes and seven heel heights. A customer can go online, create an original shoe design and then order her very own custom pair of shoes. Over 5 million pairs of shoes and counting have been designed and saved using the company's Web-based 3D-design software.

While Shoes of Prey had success, with many customers choosing to design their shoes, buy swatch samples and then order online, the founders knew by listening to their customers that many women wanted to touch the shoes, know what they'd feel like on their feet, and see how they'd look in real life. To address that need, Shoes of Prey opened their first store (within the David Jones department store in Sydney) in January 2013, earning double the forecasted revenue in their first year of operation. That same year, the startup also won the World Retail Award for the world's best store design in their category, against stiff competition from established brands like Lagerfeld and Puma. In November 2014, Shoes of Prey launched in the U.S. at Nordstrom Seattle, and five more boutiques within Nordstrom department stores are planned across the U.S.

As a more established brand now, Shoes of Prey still very much operates around a culture of what Jodie calls 'listening to her'. Their customers' wants and needs are always top of mind in every decision the company makes, from hiring and training staff to launching new products. There is also a strong culture of listening to the employees who are closest to customers in what Jodie calls 'the corners of the company'. Six years in, Shoes of Prey still surveys customers every day because as a company, they believe that the only way to show your customers that you're building a brand they can trust is to listen to what they care about.

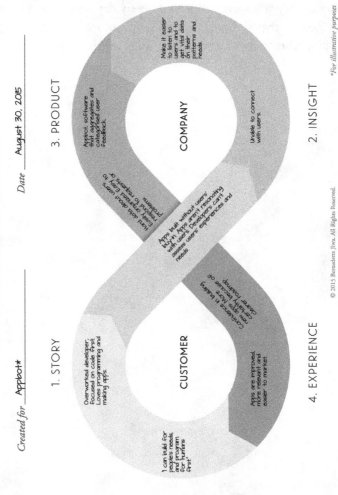

THE STORY STRATEGY BLUEPRINT

Created for ___Appbot*___   Date ___August 30, 2015___

3. PRODUCT

Make it easier to listen to users and to get vital data on their patterns and needs

Appbot: software that aggregates and categorizes user feedback

COMPANY

Unable to connect with users

2. INSIGHT

Apps that without users buy in. Apps aren't responding with users. Developers can't assess users' experiences and needs

hard and about users. Users aren't engaged. Easy to ignore problems or

1. STORY

Overworked developer. Focused on code first. Loves programming and making apps

CUSTOMER

Apps are improved, more relevant and easier to market

4. EXPERIENCE

Confidence in building apps. More in control because of clearer roadmap

"I can build for people's needs and program for humans first"

90

© 2015 Bernadette Jiwa. All Rights Reserved.

*For illustrative purposes

APPBOT

As an app developer, Stuart Hall knew that customer reviews of his product could make or break it. He took user feedback very seriously, checking reviews every day to make sure that he understood what people loved about the app he was building and how it could be improved.

Reviews of apps were difficult to collect, however, since they came from different countries, and there wasn't an easy way to reply to reviewers. So in an attempt to make better use of the data, Stuart created an application, called Appbot, that would send him his app reviews each day. After showing it to colleagues, he published a blog post about it, made it available as a free service, incorporated feedback from users, and watched its use spread through word of mouth.

Stuart knew he was onto something when he started getting emails from people asking how they could pay him for the service. It wasn't just indie app developers who started using Appbot; soon, big brands like Twitter and Evernote came on board, along with established gaming companies, who also loved how it helped them discover what was important to their users.

Appbot made it easier for developers to listen to users and not just aim for the tech PR hype of being featured in *Hacker News* one day, only to be obsolete the next because they were building things that people didn't actually want. Stuart's goal for the business was to make the data accessible and useful and to help developers build loyal followings of people who loved their products.

Today Appbot has grown into a paid product that 'surfaces user sentiment, bugs and feature requests, and seamlessly pushes this feedback' to the tools that developers use to create and support their products.

Some developers can get hundreds or even thousands of reviews a day, so Appbot makes them more manageable by clustering them into topics; it also makes it easy to reply to Google Play reviews. Appbot's features save app-development companies many hours a day compared to their previous manual workflows. Appbot's customers now include Zynga, Etsy, Evernote, Tinder, Dropbox, Uber, eBay, WordPress and Nest.

THE STORY STRATEGY BLUEPRINT

Created for ___Black Milk Clothing*___ *Date* ___March 21, 2015___

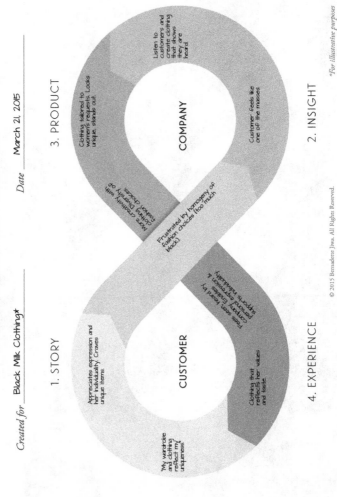

1. STORY

3. PRODUCT

2. INSIGHT

4. EXPERIENCE

COMPANY

CUSTOMER

Clothing tailored to women's requests. Looks unique, stands out.

Listen to customers and create clothing that shows they are heard.

Customer- Feels like one of the masses

More creativity with clothing. Diversity of fashion choices.

Frustrated by homogeny of fashion choices (too much black!)

Feels seen & heard by Company. Expression & fashion supports individuality.

Clothing that reflects her values and taste.

Appreciates expression and her individuality. Craves unique items.

"My wardrobe and clothing reflect my uniqueness"

*For illustrative purposes

BLACK MILK CLOTHING

James Lillis really had no right to be thinking about developing a fashion brand. He had not worked in fashion and had never run any kind of business before. On top of that, he was broke and struggling just to make his rent. What started out as a hobby—learning to sew, on a second-hand sewing machine that James pawned a CD player to buy, and taking lessons at local sewing machine shops on weekends— became the seed of a business in 2009 and a multimillion-dollar global brand in the years that followed. How did James go from nothing to creating the beloved fashion brand Black Milk Clothing?

It all started with a blog and a piece of stretchy fabric. In 2009 James sold his first pair of handmade leggings for $10 and began writing a blog called *Too Many Tights*. He quickly got a following of young women who chatted to him about how boring legwear was—black, black and more black. Legwear just wasn't helping them to express their individuality. For a whole year, James blogged and listened, going out of his way to understand what was frustrating women about fashion that made them look like everyone else.

When James eventually started scaling his business, he designed and made short product runs out of necessity because there was no big pot of money to invest in inventory. He made a pair of leggings, sold them and made another two pairs with the profit. He scaled his business one delighted wearer at a time and created an online community of young women who followed his blog. Black Milk's designs were so unusual that their customers inevitably became walking advertisements for the brand. There is no better marketing than the question 'Where did you get those?'

Black Milk's unique designs started getting attention in the press, and the business took off. But it isn't PR that's sustained the business; what makes Black Milk successful is the loyal following of their customers. When the company launches a new product, they simply leverage the power of the connection asset they have built by using permission marketing techniques and social media platforms like Instagram (where they have a million followers to date) and Facebook (almost 700,000 likers).

Even though the business has grown to become a global brand, James and his head of marketing still organise meetups and events for their brand evangelists (called 'Sharkies') and still make time to meet them. They know their customers' names and social media profiles; getting closer to their customers and understanding what they want is baked into the company's DNA. With private Facebook groups based on geographic locations and interests, Black Milk facilitates connections and friendships among the women who buy their products.

New products are previewed on social media channels like Pinterest to get feedback from customers before launch day. Each product design has an associated hashtag which customers use on social media, thus allowing their images to show up on product pages on the company's website. The women who buy the leggings are made stars of the stories. Black Milk takes pride in putting their customers front and centre, first, last and always. The intimacy they have with the women who wear their products is hard to replicate, and that priceless asset is what powers the company's continued success.

THE STORY STRATEGY BLUEPRINT

Created for _Canva_   Date _September 6, 2015_

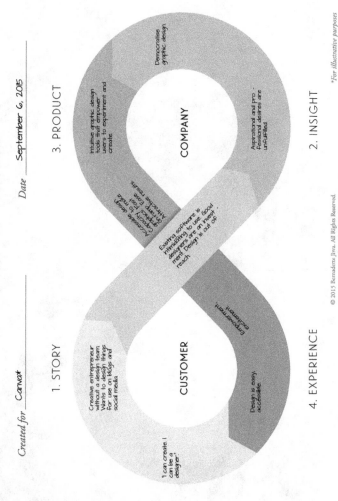

3. PRODUCT

Intuitive graphic design tools that empower users to experiment and create

Democratise graphic design

COMPANY

Aspirational and pro-fessional desires are un-fulfilled

2. INSIGHT

Existing software is intimidating to use designers are an elite, merit Design is out of reach

Increasing demand for 'do it yourself' online tools and design

1. STORY

Creative entrepreneur without a design team Wants to design things for use on blogs and social media

CUSTOMER

Design is easy, accessible.

Empowerment excitement

'I can create I can be a designer'

4. EXPERIENCE

*For illustrative purposes

98

CANVA

While studying design at university, Melanie Perkins also taught the subject to students from different departments. She noticed that it took students so long to learn the basics of the existing design programs that they made little progress in a whole semester. Instead of helping users to communicate visually, the tools simply frustrated them. The insights Melanie gathered from watching people who knew little or nothing about design and the tools designers use became the foundation for Canva.

Melanie wanted to create a product that would democratise design. She set about building a tool that would make design more accessible to more people who were not experts on the tools but who wanted and needed to design. A year into developing the software, Melanie and her team did some user testing and noticed that users were scared to click on things, so 'they wandered around aimlessly, struggled with a few things, created something that looked pretty average and then left feeling dejected.'

Watching what users did gave rise to an epiphany. It wasn't just the graphic design tools that had to be changed; Canva also 'needed to empower people who weren't graphic designers to believe they could design'. If Canva was to succeed, the team had to find a way to make sure people had a great experience the first time they used the program. So the team 'spent months perfecting the onboarding experience, paying particular attention to users' emotional journey'. The onboarding process was designed to help people master the tools quickly and to encourage them to believe that they didn't need to be professional designers to get great results.

Canva also created a world-class customer support team that is available twenty-four hours a day to help solve users' problems and has an average response time of two hours. The team generates a daily 'customer happiness report' that summarises the issues that arose and were resolved. By delighting users, exceeding expectations and generating goodwill, Canva has grown to a community of 2.8 million users in just twenty months.

THE STORY STRATEGY BLUEPRINT

Created for ___Flow Hive*___ *Date* ___December 13, 2015___

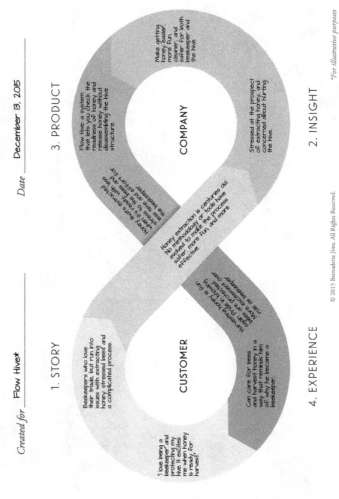

1. STORY

3. PRODUCT

2. INSIGHT

4. EXPERIENCE

COMPANY

Make getting honey easier, more fun, cleaner, and safer for both beekeeper and the hive

Flow Hive a system that lets you check the readiness of honey and release honey without disassembling the hive structure

Stressed at the prospect of extracting honey, and concerned about hurting the hive

Honey extraction is centuries old. No methodology or tools have evolved to make the tools have safer, more fun, and process effective more

CUSTOMER

Beekeepers who love their trade, but run into issues with extracting honey, stressed bees and a complicated process

"I love being a beekeeper and protecting my hive. It excites me when honey is ready for harvest."

Can care for bees and harvest honey in a way that reminds him of why he became a beekeeper

For illustrative purposes

FLOW HIVE

As seasoned beekeepers, Stuart and Cedar Anderson knew firsthand the drawbacks and sometimes the perils of harvesting honey from hives. The process of donning the protective gear, disturbing and smoking the bees, removing the frames, brushing the bees off the honeycombs, removing the wax capping from the frames, extracting the honey and then putting the hive back together, often squashing bees in the process, wasn't what you could call a walk in the park. While harvesting the honey was part and parcel of the labour of love for them and their fellow beekeepers, the father and son did wonder why the way they did it hadn't evolved for more than a century.

This understanding of the day-to-day challenges that faced beekeepers was what inspired the Andersons to 'set to work on a decade long task of inventing the beekeeper's dream'. They created and patented a system that lets the beekeeper see into the hive to check whether the honey is ready, and to do this without disturbing the bees. The extraction system makes collecting honey less stressful for both the bees and the beekeeper. Now it's possible to use a tool that allows honey to be released from the special frames without anyone's cracking open the hive.

Flow Hive literally allows beekeepers to have honey on tap. And this honey needs no filtering, heating or any kind of processing—as the Andersons put it on Indiegogo, it's 'pure, clean (no wax [or] bee bits) and extra tasty!'

In their campaign story, the Andersons didn't just present the facts about their invention; they also understood that beekeepers still wanted the feeling of being connected to the bees and being involved in the process. The Andersons were able to solve a practical problem for beekeepers but still consider their emotional needs, saying 'we haven't taken all the fun away. You still get to use your smoker and beekeeper suit and do all the normal things to keep your bees healthy.'

When their invention was finally patented and ready, they launched a crowdfunding campaign on Indiegogo to bring Flow Hive to market. Within an hour of their launch, they had blasted through the $100,000 goal. By the end of the first day, the project had set an Indiegogo record for the most funds raised on day one: $2.1 million.

The Flow Hive campaign raised a total of $12.4 million from more than 36,000 backers—another Indiegogo record.

THE STORY STRATEGY BLUEPRINT

Created for ___GoPro*___   Date ___January 10. 2015___

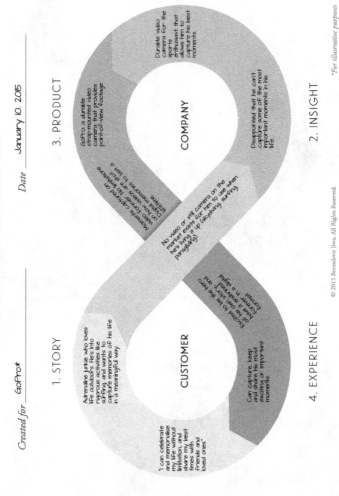

3. PRODUCT

Durable video camera for the sports enthusiast that allows him to capture his best moments

GoPro: a durable strap-mounted video camera that provides point-of-view footage

COMPANY

Disappointed that he can't capture some of the most important moments in his life.

2. INSIGHT

1. STORY

Adrenaline junkie who loves life outdoors. He's into rigorous activities like surfing and wants to capture memories of his life in a meaningful way.

No video or still camera on the market exists for him to use when he's living it up (skydiving, surfing, paragliding)

Moments captured on video become timeless and memories to last a lifetime

CUSTOMER

'I can celebrate and memorialise my life without limitation and share my best exciting or important times with friends and loved ones'

Can capture, keep and share his most exciting or important moments

Edited to tell the hero or the story and have it archived forever in a digital format

4. EXPERIENCE

© 2015 Bernadette Jiwa. All Rights Reserved.

*For illustrative purposes

106

GOPRO

In 2002, following the failure of his second online business during the dot-com bust, Nick Woodman planned a five-month surfing trip to Australia and Indonesia to work out how he could continue on his entrepreneurial journey. As he told *Around the World in 80 Brands*, the inspiration for GoPro came before he left: he couldn't find a camera that would let him take close-up photos of himself and his friends while they were surfing, so he set out to develop a wrist harness into which he could put a single-use disposable camera, which would in theory do the trick.

The straps he sewed did work, but the cameras he tried did not—they couldn't withstand water or the impact of extreme sports. Knowing that other surfers would want the same kind of camera setup that he did—a setup that didn't exist—he decided to build a camera company that would focus on meeting the needs of the everyday extreme-action videographer.

It took Nick two years to find a waterproof camera that was close to what he wanted. Then he persuaded the Chinese manufacturer of that camera to adapt it to accommodate a strap mount.

Built with just $265,000 of capital, GoPro officially got off the ground with its first order for 100 cameras at an action-sports trade show in 2004, with Nick as the single employee.

The company's first digital model didn't launch until 2006. The timing for entry into the video camera market was perfect, as Google bought YouTube in 2006 and the demand for an inexpensive camera that could shoot high-quality action footage grew. The GoPro let even inexperienced camera operators and adrenaline junkies become the heroes of their own stories, which they naturally wanted to share. This, it turned out, was the best marketing a company could hope for—customers in the thousands showing friends the experiences that the GoPro captured.

Following its IPO in June 2014, GoPro was valued at $2.96 billion.

THE STORY STRATEGY BLUEPRINT

Created for __Little Flowers*__ Date __May 3, 2015__

1. STORY

3. PRODUCT

2. INSIGHT

4. EXPERIENCE

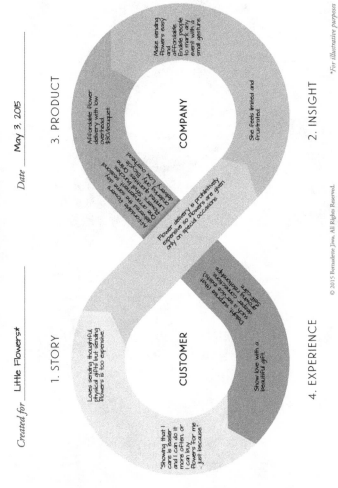

COMPANY

Make sending flowers easy and affordable. Enable people to mark any event with a small gesture.

Affordable flower delivery with low overhead. $20/bouquet

She feels limited and frustrated

Flower delivery is prohibitively expensive so flowers are given only on special occasions

CUSTOMER

Loves sending thoughtful physical gifts but sending flowers is too expensive

Show love with a beautiful gift

Showing that I care is easier and I can do it more often or I can buy flowers for me - just because

For illustrative purposes

LITTLE FLOWERS

Sending someone you care about some pretty flowers to let them know you are thinking of them should be about the gesture and not the dollar amount spent. That's what the team at Little Flowers in Sydney believed. As romantics, flower lovers and givers, they knew that people adored giving and receiving flowers; they also knew that the cost of sending them (based on wastage and overhead in the business) prohibited spontaneous flower giving. This meant that even people who wanted to send flowers did so only once or twice a year.

That fact got Sarah Regan and her co-founder, Chris Berents, thinking about how they could take the 'bigness' out of the flower industry and help people get all of the joy of giving and receiving flowers by making it about the gesture. There didn't seem to be a product or service that bridged the gap between the extravagant $100 bouquet ordered from a traditional florist and the bunch of tired roses hastily picked up from the petrol station forecourt. Sarah and her team set out to change all that was broken in the traditional model and make flower giving all about the gesture.

The Little Flowers team simplified things and cut costs (without compromising on delight and quality) by removing the expensive shopfront. They reduced waste by selling one type of seasonal, pre-ordered bouquet daily in limited quantities for $30 including delivery. They covered urban areas that were easier for bicycle couriers to access and deliver to in batches.

All of these changes lowered overheads, enabling Little Flowers to pass those savings on to delighted customers, who in turn were happy to spread the word. Every little bunch was a tiny billboard for the company, and word-of-mouth marketing led to Little Flowers becoming the fastest-growing online florist in Australia.

Along the way, the team gained some valuable insights about their customers. Women want to send flowers to other women and to themselves (just because). Little Flowers are a small indulgence. Now people don't need a big excuse to send flowers, no moment needs to go uncelebrated, and there need never be another embarrassed office worker wrestling a gigantic bouquet of flowers on public transport as she heads home from work.

Sarah and her co-founders haven't just built a sustainable business; they have become a beloved brand that's recognised and loved throughout the city.

THE STORY STRATEGY BLUEPRINT

Created for ___Khan Academy___   Date ___February 18, 2015___

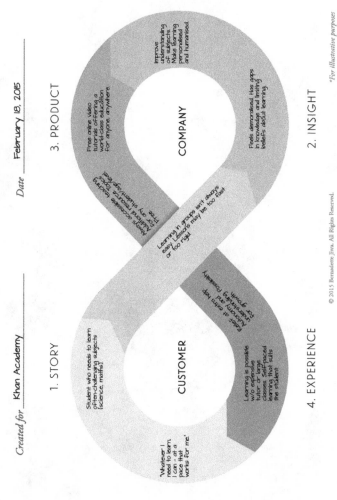

1. STORY

3. PRODUCT

2. INSIGHT

4. EXPERIENCE

COMPANY

CUSTOMER

Free online video tutorials offering a world-class education for anyone anywhere

Improve understanding of subjects. Make learning personalised and humanised

Always accessible and without cost. For school subjects (K-12)

Learning in groups isn't always easy or I don't always learn at the right pace. Lessons may be too fast or too slight.

Feels demoralised. Has apps in knowledge and limiting beliefs about learning

Student who needs to learn often-challenging subjects (science, maths)

Reach at extra help. Understanding and the funds necessary for growth

"Whatever I need to learn, I can - at a pace that works for me"

Learning is possible w/o expensive tutor or large classes. Self-paced learning that suits the student

KHAN ACADEMY

In 2004, Salman (Sal) Khan, a hedge fund analyst living in Boston, began helping his cousins, who lived in New Orleans, with maths, tutoring them remotely via the Internet. He started off using Yahoo Doodle and a phone. It wasn't until 2006 that he decided, after some prodding from a friend, to create videos of the lessons he recorded and put them on YouTube.

Sal soon discovered that his cousins preferred video-lesson Sal to real-time Sal. When he began to dig into the reasons, they weren't all that surprising. Now that his cousins could pause, repeat and review the lessons, they could go over the parts they needed extra help with and refresh their memories. And as Sal said in his TED Talk in 2011, 'the very first time that you're trying to get your brain around a new concept, the very last thing you need is another human being saying, "Do you understand this?"'

Other people stumbled onto Sal's videos on YouTube and found them helpful. They began commenting about the impact the videos had on their understanding of the topics they were studying. Many viewers talked about having a breakthrough or enjoying the subject for the first time.

As Sal's audience grew, to his surprise he started getting emails from teachers who were using his lessons to 'humanize the classroom' by flipping the traditional lecture-style teaching model on its head. '[R]emoving the one-size-fits-all lecture from the classroom' allowed the students to pace their learning by watching Sal's video lessons at home before coming to school. Because students were familiar with the material, teachers could help them in more practical ways during class time, bridging gaps in their understanding and tailoring their teaching to each student's ability and current level of understanding.

In 2009, Sal decided to quit his day job to focus on developing his online teaching platform, Khan Academy (a non-profit), which was clearly changing the lives of thousands of students and teachers and had the potential to reinvent and humanise education. His goal was to change the traditional model, which he says 'penalizes you for experimentation and failure, but ... does not expect mastery'. Khan Academy was designed to do the opposite and to 'arm teachers with as much data as possible ... so [they] can ... make their interaction [with each student] as productive as possible'.

Sal's vision for a 'global one-world classroom', where parents, teachers and students are empowered, has become a reality. From one man using a computer in a closet at home, Khan Academy has grown into an 80-person team that has built 'a personalized learning resource for all ages' with 26 million registered students. The academy teaches maths, biology, chemistry, physics, computer programming, history, art history, healthcare and economics, using instructional videos and practice exercises, and provides dashboards for both students and coaches. There are Spanish, Brazilian Portuguese, and French versions of the website, and resources are being translated into thirty-six additional languages.

Khan Academy removes the fear of not knowing the right answer, perpetuated by traditional teaching and testing methods, and gives students the confidence to believe that their understanding will come with time and effort.

As the landing page on their website says: 'You only have to know one thing: You can learn anything.'

THE STORY STRATEGY BLUEPRINT

Created for ___Harry's*___   Date ___August 10, 2015___

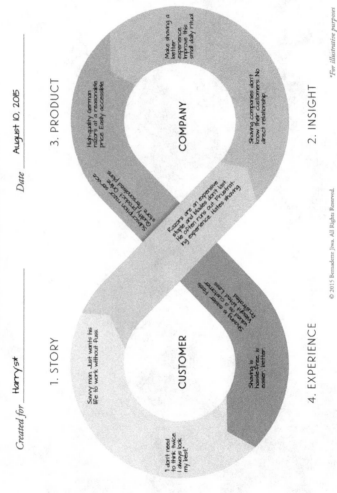

1. STORY

3. PRODUCT

2. INSIGHT

4. EXPERIENCE

COMPANY

CUSTOMER

High-quality German razors at a reasonable price. Easily accessible

Subscription razor and blade (no razor) for sale. Personalized plans

Make shaving a better experience. Improve this small daily ritual

Shaving companies don't know their customers. No direct relationship

Razors are an expensive staple and blades don't last. He often runs out. Frustrating experience. Hates shaving

Savvy man. Just wants his life to work without fuss

Shaving is basic. Price is easy, better

Payment is a barrier. Wants a barrier-free customer experience

"I don't need to think twice. I always look my best"

*For illustrative purposes

HARRY'S

Harry's is a men's grooming brand founded by Andy Katz-Mayfield and Jeff Raider in 2013. The company sells high-quality razors and shaving products directly to men for half the price of major brands.

The idea for Harry's came after Andy had a frustrating visit to the drugstore to pick up some razors. He waited ten minutes for someone to unlock the cabinet where the razors were kept, paid $25 for four razors and some shaving cream and left feeling ripped-off. As Jeff, also a co-founder of Warby Parker, said in an interview with ThriveWire, 'Andy called [him] with the idea for Harry's and the conviction that "there has to be a better way".' Then the researching and testing began:

> Andy and I tried every shaving product we could get our hands on—for each product we reviewed the purchasing experience, the price and the quality. There was nothing on the market that satisfied all three of these areas for us. We also spent a lot of time talking to anyone and everyone (friends, family, colleagues) about their shaving habits, and product preferences.
> —*Jeff Raider, co-founder, Harry's*

Razors are something that most men use every day; shaving is part of their routine, a daily ritual, and yet most men don't love doing it. It clearly wasn't just the purchase experience that was broken; blade quality was lacking, too. Andy and Jeff knew from friends in the industry that big brands spend millions of dollars on research and development, intellectual property, sponsorship and marketing. What Andy and Jeff discovered was that good razor blades are hard to make; at one stage, they thought they might have to abandon the idea, until they found a ninety-four-year-old factory in Germany to partner with (they went on to buy the factory and now devote significant resources to R&D and IP themselves).

Andy and Jeff understood that men hated shaving and were frustrated with the products they had to use every single day. The big brands were charging a lot for a product that wasn't that convenient to buy or great to use. When they launched Harry's, Andy and Jeff wanted to 'make the whole process of shaving ... easier and more approachable and ... more enjoyable'.

Because Harry's has a direct relationship with customers, they get incredible feedback. The company regards feedback as a gift that helps them to learn and get better. Unlike their competitors, Harry's knows who is buying their product and how often, and they see that as an opportunity to create value by delivering a better and more personal experience. The sale of the product is just the start of the relationship; Harry's emails all of their customers to ask how they are doing and to make sure they are happy with the products. The direct relationship is one of the keys to the brand's success and a definite competitive advantage. Customers sometimes suggest features or make requests, and the Harry's team categorises feedback and uses it to drive the company's R&D.

Harry's offers a 'starter set' with basic supplies for $15. Over time, Harry's can tailor their offerings to men in a more personal way based on how often they shave and the kinds of products they buy and how often. As Jeff says, 'the better we know you, the better we can make that experience'. And what he learned from his time at Warby Parker was, 'It's about figuring out what the customer wants and how best to deliver them a great brand experience.'

While Harry's launched into a highly competitive marketplace against players with huge marketing budgets, and did so with some excellent PR and reviews from men's fashion editors, it's organic growth and word of mouth that are powering the brand's continued success.

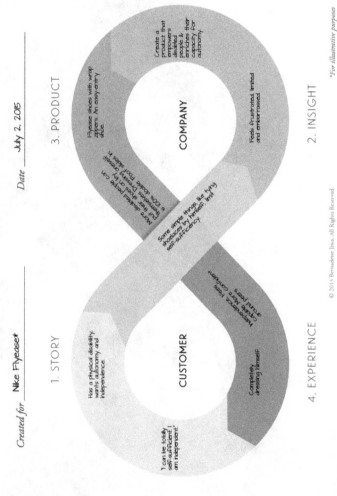

THE STORY STRATEGY BLUEPRINT

Created for Nike Flyease*   *Date* July 2, 2015

1. STORY

3. PRODUCT

2. INSIGHT

4. EXPERIENCE

CUSTOMER

COMPANY

BERNADETTE JIWA

*For illustrative purposes

NIKE FLYEASE

Matthew Walzer had learned to overcome many of the challenges that confronted him daily because of his cerebral palsy. There was one simple thing that he wanted to do but couldn't, and it affected his life every day, so three years ago, at age sixteen, he wrote to Nike asking for help.

> Out of all the challenges I have overcome in my life, there is one that I am still trying to master, tying my shoes. Cerebral palsy stiffens the muscles in the body. As a result I have flexibility in only one of my hands which makes it impossible for me to tie my shoes. My dream is to go to the college of my choice without having to worry about someone coming to tie my shoes every day.
>
> ... At 16 years old, I am able to completely dress myself, but my parents still have to tie my shoes. As a teenager who is striving to become totally self-sufficient, I find this extremely frustrating, and at times, embarrassing.

Nike responded by not only creating a pair of shoes for Matthew, but also asking him to work with them to develop an 'easy-entry shoe' that could empower more disabled people to develop greater independence.

Nike's renowned designer Tobie Hatfield teamed up with Matthew, and after three years of research and development, the 'Flyease' was born. By talking to Matthew and other people with disabilities, Hatfield discovered that the shoes needed two things: ease of entry and a closing system that didn't require fine motor movement like lacing a traditional shoe did.

The Flyease shoe looks like a traditional basketball shoe with ankle support, but it has a 'wrap-around zipper ... that opens the back of the shoe near the heel-counter, making it easier to slide the foot in and out. At the same time, the system provides sufficient lockdown and eliminates the need to tie traditional laces.'

Because Nike listened to and acted on his story, Matthew Walzer is now attending college and has the ability to do something most of us take for granted every day. The company has a product people want, which they have now made available to other athletes with disabilities, and Nike is continuing to research and develop other styles in the Flyease range.

CONCLUSION:
CLOSE, CLOSER, CLOSEST

Go out and find some real people. Listen to their stories. Don't ask for the main point. Let the story run its course. Like flowing water, it will find its own way, at its own pace. And if you've got patience, you'll learn more than you might imagine.
—Tom Kelley, General Manager, IDEO

INTENTION AND CERTAINTY

How did the founders of Blue Apron, the meal kit delivery service, know for certain their idea would work? Did Amy Cuddy realise before she nervously walked out to deliver her TED Talk in 2012 that her idea and the way she shared it would resonate so much that it would become the second-most-watched TED Talk of all time or that a book deal would follow? Could the inventors of Flow Hive have predicted the outstanding $12 million success of their Indiegogo campaign? What would have happened back in the early days if Airbnb co-founder Brian Chesky had taken to heart the statement 'I hope you're working on something else' from a trusted advisor?

There is no way of knowing how well an idea will resonate before launch day. You can understand the problem to solve, conduct surveys, do usability testing, hold focus groups and ask advice from those who have gone before you, but the only way to know for sure is to put the idea out there and let the people you create for decide if it's worthy of their time, attention, money or love. We can't be certain what people will do until we allow them to do it.

It takes courage to be the person who cares enough to design your work and life around failing in order to succeed. In truth, failing at some point is the one thing you can count on. If there were such a thing as a 'sure thing', a hundred and one other people would already have done what you're planning to do—and that would make it commonplace, not meaningful, which is what you are shooting for.

A SILVER BULLET OR THE SMALLEST THING

In our own quest for significance and success, it's easy to fall into the trap of thinking that what our customers, audiences and communities want (and will pay for) are complex solutions to their big problems. What they really want, in fact, is to be helped to do the things they want to do. They may just want thoughtful solutions to ordinary problems. The smallest thing can feel like magic to someone who has been living with a problem they may not be able to articulate.

As I was putting this book to bed and considering deleting this section because I thought I'd said all of this before, I came across the story of a young man who lives in Tehran (posted by Brandon Stanton of Humans of New York on Instagram).

My mother died when I was two years old, so it's just me and my father. He's been really angry with me lately. He's always wanted me to be an engineer like him, but I switched my major to photography. He didn't show any emotion when I told him. He always has a poker face ... I know he's angry at me from the little things. He never asks me to go shopping with him anymore. We used to go to the market together. He'd pick up a watermelon, inspect it, then would hand it to me for my opinion. It doesn't sound like much but I really valued that time together ... [O]nce I changed my major he stopped asking me to come along. But I think things are getting better. Recently I scored top 5th percentile on the University Entrance Exam for photography. When I told my father he didn't show any emotion. But the next day he asked me if I wanted to go shopping. And that made me so happy. Because it's just the two of us. And I really, really, really, really love him.

The things people want deep down, which are the building blocks of our businesses, are smaller and closer than we think. And sometimes they have nothing to do with business and everything to do with reminding us of our humanity.

SHOW THEM THEIR WINGS

When we have worked hard to bring something to the world, it's natural to want to shout about it. All the effort, blood, sweat and tears start to pay off only after the idea is past the incubation stage and 'out there', interacting with its intended market. It's so tempting to feel like we are finished on launch day because of the work we've put in behind the scenes for weeks, months or even years that the customer never sees, and it's so easy to fall into the trap of just shouting about what we've created. We naturally want to say, 'Look at this amazing thing I made; can you see how incredibly awesome it is? Can you sense the agonising that's gone into every decision it took to bring it to life, the long days, the sleepless nights?' On launch day and beyond, we feel like it's time for the world to sit up and take notice. But with so many things out there to notice, why should the world pay attention to you and why will it want to?

You don't need all of the world on day one, and let's take that one step further—you positively don't want the attention of the whole world, because that means you've made something for everyone, not something that's going to be loved by the people you want to matter to first. When we stop saying, 'Look at the incredible wings we've made for you' and begin with, 'Can you see how amazing your wings are in this light?' it changes everything.

The trap we fall into is trying to tell people how life-changing our widget is. If it changes their lives, we won't have to tell them.

SUCCEED WILDLY

Try not to become a person of success, but rather try to become a person of value.
—ALBERT EINSTEIN

Nobody sets out to be average. We all want to matter—to know that our work made a difference and that our time counted for something. One of the best ways to do that is to look outside ourselves—to make others feel like they matter.

The story of ideas that fly is really the story of the people who adopt them. It's how their narratives and the realisation of their hopes, dreams and aspirations collide with what we create that makes an innovation meaningful or helps an idea take off.

Start there. Create generously, succeed wildly—show us our wings.

USING THE STORY STRATEGY BLUEPRINT

Our task is to read things that are not yet on the page.
—STEVE JOBS

I hope this book has inspired you to start anew to understand your customer's story and to make your ideas fly. I am adding this 'guidelines' section at the end of the book so that you can read the book all the way through and then begin implementing the Story Strategy Blueprint when you're ready.

You can download both the blueprint and a stripped-down working version at meaningfulbook.com.

If you'd like to know more about joining me and other entrepreneurs and business leaders in a group program designed to guide you through the process, please contact me or sign up for more details at thestorystrategy.com.

Let's take a look at the blueprint together and walk through the four sections.

1. STORY

Begin in the top left-hand corner of the blueprint, at #1 STORY.

Think about who your customer is beyond basic demographics like sex, age and income. Describe a day in her life as fully as possible.

What is her worldview?

What does she care about?

How does she spend her days?

What problems does she encounter?

2. INSIGHT

Use the bottom right-hand corner of the blueprint to document your understanding about what she wants to do—but can't—and start thinking about how your products and services might help her.

Where do you have the opportunity to make the most difference to her?

These insights may reveal valuable information about possible ideas for products and services, as well as ways to scale and market them.

3. PRODUCT

Follow the loop back up to the top right to the 3. PRODUCT section.

Information gained in 2. INSIGHTS will inform the kinds of products, services and marketing you create for your customers. Think in terms of both rational and emotional benefits, tangible and intangible value.

What features and benefits are required to help solve your customer's problem?

How will using your product or service make her feel?

4. EXPERIENCE

Lastly, follow on from 3. PRODUCT to 4. EXPERIENCE in the bottom left corner of the blueprint. Think about how you want your customer to experience your product or service. Walk through the customer's journey from awareness to affinity and from purchase to evangelism. Consider every touchpoint and the effect your product has on how your customer feels and how she perceives herself.

What's changed for your customer as a result of using your product? For example, the Shoes of Prey customer with larger feet who previously couldn't find a pair of great shoes to fit her now feels more feminine. She walks taller (literally and metaphorically) and has more confidence.

The insights you glean from assessing how your customer's perceptions have changed help you improve your products and services, recognise opportunities to create new products for your customer and better serve her.

Which takes you back to #1 on the Story Strategy Blueprint: the ideation phase.

THE BREAKING POINT

On the original Story Strategy Blueprint, you will notice a dotted line that indicates the 'breaking point'; this is where many companies fail to use insights about their customers and translate those insights into features and benefits that truly serve them. Companies often create customer profiles—describing customers' stories, wants and needs—at the beginning of the product creation process but then drop them midway through the research and development process. This in turn leads to the unhelpful marketing cycle of working hard to make people want things, instead of making things that people want.

REFERENCES

THE STORY OF THIS BOOK

'We really need to care…' — Bjarke Ingels, Danish architect, in the video 'Advice to the Young'. <https://www.youtube.com/watch?v=8yMzZwAtZRw>

The customer is the starting point — Peter Drucker, *Management: Tasks, Responsibilities, Practices.* (NY: Harper & Row, 1973.)

PART 1: THE RELEVANCE REVOLUTION

THE BEFORE AND THE AFTER

'Start with the customer experience' — 'Steve Jobs on Apple Customer Experience and Innovation', YouTube. <https://www.youtube.com/watch?v=i7LiR5QqoNA>

'Who do you want…' — Michael Schrage, *Who Do You Want Your Customer to Become?* Harvard Business Review Press, 17 July 2012.

PERFECTING THE WINGS

His paper plane model — Sean Hutchinson, 'The Perfect Paper Airplane', *Mental_floss,* 14 January 2014. <http://mentalfloss.com/article/54488/perfect-paper-airplane>

THE RELEVANCE ENGINE

'The best inventions…' and 'the most popular search query' — Eric Schmidt, 'The New Gründergeist'. Google | Europe blog, 13 October 2014. <http://googlepolicyeurope.blogspot.com.au/2014/10/the-new-grundergeist.html>

CAUSE AND EFFECT

'Get closer than ever to your customers' — Steve Jobs, quoted by Ekaterina Walter, '40 Eye-Opening Customer Service Quotes'. *Forbes*, 4 March 2014. <http://www.forbes.com/sites/ekaterinawalter/2014/03/04/40-eye-opening-customer-service-quotes/>

WE DON'T NEED BETTER MARKETING

Quotations describing the Mr Kipling packaging changes — 'Mr Kipling demonstrates "Life Is Better With Cake" With Significant Investment Over the Next 12 Months'. *Premier Foods*, 26 August 2014. <http://www.premierfoods.co.uk/media/news-features/Items/Mr-Kipling-demonstrates-%E2%80%98Life-Is-Better-With-Cake%E2%80%99>

THE LEGACY TRAP

Newspaper advertising fell — Bourree Lam, 'Newspaper Ad Revenue Fell $40 Billion in a Decade'. *The Atlantic,* 23 October 2014. <http://www.theatlantic.com/business/archive/2014/10/newspaper-ad-revenue-fell-40-billion-in-a-decade/381732/>

'Editors and producers pursued…' — Robert G. Kaiser, 'The Bad News'. *The Brookings Essay*, 16 October 2014. <http://www.brookings.edu/research/essays/2014/bad-news#>

BuzzFeed statistics — 'Custom Content Worth Sharing', *BuzzFeed.com*, accessed in August 2015. <http://www.buzzfeed.com/advertise>

Harry's donates 1 percent… — 'Our Giving Model', Harrys.com. <https://www.harrys.com/give-a-shave>

Harry's has attracted over 100,000 customers — Tom DiChristopher, 'Online Shaving Start-Up Takes On the Big Blades'. *CNBC.com,* 10 November 2014. <http://www.cnbc.com/2014/11/10/online-shaving-start-up-takes-on-the-big-blades.html>

IMPROBABLE HEROES

'Every time one of us would get a sick barrel' — Steve Berra, 'GoPro with Founder/Inventor Nick Woodman', Company Q&A with Steve Berra, *Malakye.com*, 1 May 2010. <https://www.malakye.com/Features/CompanyQA/3518/GoPro-with-Founder-Inventor-Nick-Woodman.aspx>

General information about the development of the GoPro —

(1) Ryan Mac, 'The Mad Billionaire Behind GoPro: The World's Hottest Camera Company'. *Forbes*, 25 March 2013. <http://www.forbes.com/sites/ryanmac/2013/03/04/the-mad-billionaire-behind-gopro-the-worlds-hottest-camera-company/>

(2) The Cam Authority, 'History of the GoPro'. <http://www.goprobuyersguide.com/story>

(3) Robert Moritz, 'Guts, Glory, and Megapixels: The Story of GoPro.' *Popular Mechanics*, 12 June 2012. <http://www.popularmechanics.com/adventure/sports/a7703/guts-glory-and-megapixels-the-story-of-gopro-8347639/>

GoPro was valued at $2.96 billion — Leslie Picker, 'GoPro Jumps After IPO Values Camera Maker at $3 Billion'. *Bloomberg* Business, 26 June 2014. <http://www.bloomberg.com/news/2014-06-25/gopro-raises-427-million-pricing-ipo-at-top-of-marketed-range.html>

GoPro's late-to-market competitors — DL Cade, 'JVC and Sony Going After GoPro Market With New and Upcoming Action Cams'. *PetaPixel*, 30 June 2012. <http://petapixel.com/2012/06/30/jvc-and-sony-going-after-gopro-market-with-new-and-upcoming-action-cams/>

Sony Music missed out on creating the iPod — David Aker, 'Why Sony Missed the iPod—The Curse of Silos'. *MediaPost*, 6 February 2009. <http://www.mediapost.com/publications/article/99726/why-sony-missed-the-ipod-the-curse-of-silos.html>

THE MEANING BUSINESS

'Don't compete for the moment' — Brian Solis and @GapingVoid, 'What If PR Stood for People and Relationships? A Manifesto for Building Relationships in the Digital Era', slide 26. *Slideshare.net*, 14 December 2014. <http://www.briansolis.com/2014/10/manifesto-building-relationships-digital-era/>

When the Apple store first opened — 'Ron Johnson: Trust in Your Imagination and Instinct'. Interview published on *YouTube*, 28 May 2014. <https://www.youtube.com/watch?v=e_HByVsugQY>

The Apple Store took a few years to catch on — Lisa Eadicicco, 'What It Was Like to Create the Apple Store, According to the Man Who Helped Steve Jobs Build It'. *Business Insider*, 19 June 2015. <http://www.businessinsider.com/ron-johnson-apple-store-steve-jobs-2015-6>

The most successful retail concept — David Lidsky, 'Apple Alum Ron Johnson Is Giving His Employees the Best of Both the Gig Economy & Traditional Employment'. *Fast Company*, 14 May 2015. <http://www.fastcompany.com/3046273/tech-forecast/apple-alum-ron-johnson-is-giving-his-employees-the-best-of-both-the-gig-econom>

'We are more than a store' — Leander Kahney, 'Apple Fans, Do You Feel Lucky?' *Wired*. 27 February 2004. <http://archive.wired.com/gadgets/mac/news/2004/02/62455>

PART 2: THE FUTURE STARTS HERE

'The future belongs…' — Daniel Pink, *A Whole New Mind: Why Right-Brainers Will Rule the Future* (New York: Penguin, 2005).

DISRUPTION HAPPENS ONE PERSON AT A TIME

'The best … measure of innovation' — Steward Butterfield, 'We Don't Sell Saddles Here'. *Medium*, 17 February 2014. <https://medium.com/@stewart/we-dont-sell-saddles-here-4c59524d650d>

Today Gillette sales… — 'The World's Most Valuable Brands', 2015 Ranking, *Forbes*. <http://www.forbes.com/companies/gillette/>

The history of shaving and Gillette — Randy Schueller, 'Safety Razor'. *How Products Are Made*. <http://www.madehow.com/Volume-5/Safety-Razor.html>

Jean-Jacques Perret's invention — Robert K. Waits, 'From Perret to Kampfe: Origins of the Safety Razor'. <http://www.shaveworld.org/home/images/PerrettKampfe-rev2.html>

SHIFTS DON'T HAPPEN BY ACCIDENT

Print-book sales fell 9 percent — Jim Milliot, 'Rate of Print Decline Flattened in 2012'. *Publishers Weekly*, 4 January 2013. < http:// www.publishersweekly.com/pw/by-topic/industry-news/bookselling/ article/55382-rate-of-print-decline-flattened-in-2012.html>

Books used to compete... — Publishing Technology PLC, 'Publishers' Association Stats Tell Story of Rising Digital Sales and a Declining Market'. *ContentForward* blog, 21 May 2014. <http://www. publishingtechnology.com/2014/05/rising-sales-declining-market-for-publishers/>

'Create as much information in two days' — MG Siegler, 'Eric Schmidt: Every 2 Days We Create As Much Information As We Did up to 2003'. *TechCrunch,* 4 August 2010. <http://techcrunch. com/2010/08/04/schmidt-data/>

KNOWING vs UNDERSTANDING

'I hope there will be fewer attempts...' — Interview in 'How Marketing Will Change in 2015: The Creative Forecast'. *Fast Company* Co.Create, 5 January 2015. <http://www.fastcocreate.com/3040028/ how-marketing-will-change-in-2015-the-creative-forecast>

'Tesco had committed to customer research...' — Michael Schrage, 'Tesco's Downfall Is a Warning to Data-Driven Retailers'. *Harvard Business Review*, 28 October 2014. <https://hbr.org/2014/10/tescos-downfall-is-a-warning-to-data-driven-retailers/>

MAKE THINGS PEOPLE WANT

'There is nothing offensive...' — 'Sir Martin Sorrell at the 2014 Media Summit'. *YouTube.* <https://www.youtube.com/watch?v=BIF9BY9l-eQ>

The IKEA business model — Beth Kowitt, 'How Ikea Took Over the World'. *Fortune,* 15 March 2015. <http://fortune.com/ikea-world-domination/>

Earthquake beams in Japanese flats — John Dawson and Masao Mukoyama, editors, *Global Strategies in Retailing: Asian and European Experiences.* Routledge, 11 September 2013.

IKEA in China — Eric Lin, 'Balancing Global and Local'. Siegel+Gale, accessed in August 2015, <http://www.siegelgale.com/balancing-global-and-local/>

Statistics about IKEA — 'The World's Most Valuable Brands', 2015 Ranking, *Forbes.* <http://www.forbes.com/companies/ikea/>

Flow Hive — 'Flow Hive: Honey on Tap Directly From Your Beehive'. <https://www.indiegogo.com/projects/flow-hive-honey-on-tap-directly-from-your-beehive>

WHERE DID THOMAS EDISON START?

'We will make electricity...' — 'Thomas Edison'. *Wikipedia.* <http://en.wikipedia.org/wiki/Thomas_Edison#cite_note-55>

Thomas Edison and the invention of the light bulb —

(1) 'Thomas Edison'. *Wikipedia.* <http://en.wikipedia.org/wiki/Thomas_Edison>

(2) Charles Hooper, 'Important Facts About Thomas Edison & the Invention of the Light Bulb'. *Synonym.com,* Demand Media. <http://classroom.synonym.com/important-thomas-edison-invention-light-bulb-6305.html>

(3) Lee Krystek, 'Surprising Science: Who Invented the Lightbulb?' *The Museum of Unnatural Mystery*. 2002 <http://www.unmuseum.org/lightbulb.htm>

(4) 'Thomas Edison: Early Life'. <http://www.schenectadymuseum.org/edison/a_timeline/01_a02.htm>

EMOTIONAL CAPITAL

'Innovation today is inextricably linked...' — Cliff Kuang, 'Why Good Design Is Finally a Bottom Line Investment'. *Fast Company*, 17 April 2015. <http://www.fastcodesign.com/1670679/good-design-is-good-business-an-introduction>

THE CONTEXT REVOLUTION

More than half of digital content — Susan Gunelius, 'More than Half of Digital Content Now Consumed on Mobile Devices'. *ACI. info*, 14 May 2014. <http://aci.info/2014/05/14/more-than-half-of-digital-content-now-consumed-on-mobile-devices/>

Disney's MagicBand — Cliff Kuang, 'Disney's $1 Billion Bet on a Magical Wristband'. *Wired*, 10 March 2015. <http://www.wired.com/2015/03/disney-magicband/>

The power of social media referrals — Mike Ewing, '71% More Likely to Purchase Based on Social Media Referrals'. *HubSpot*, 9 January 2012. <http://blog.hubspot.com/blog/tabid/6307/bid/30239/71-More-Likely-to-Purchase-Based-on-Social-Media-Referrals-Infographic.aspx>

'Individuals are able to personalize...' — 'November 2014 Trend Briefing: Post-Demographic Consumerism'. *TrendWatching.com*. <http://trendwatching.com/trends/post-demographic-consumerism/>

'Personalization and beauty are everything' — David Pierce, 'iPhone Killer: The Secret History of the Apple Watch'. *Wired*. <www.wired.com/2015/04/the-apple-watch/>

There are 80,000 drink combinations — 'Fact: There Are 80,000 Ways to Drink a Starbucks Beverage'. *The Huffington Post*, 4 March 2014. <http://www.huffingtonpost.com/2014/03/04/starbucks_n_4890735.html>

Fifteen shades of grey — '15 Shades of Prey', *Shoes of Prey.com*, accessed in August 2015. <https://www.shoesofprey.com/style-help/1825069286/15-shades-of-prey>

Millennials are less concerned about privacy — American Press Institute, 'Digital Lives of Millennials'. *How Millennials Get News: Inside the Habits of America's First Digital Generation*, 15 March 2015. <http://www.americanpressinstitute.org/publications/reports/survey-research/digital-lives-of-millennials/>

Definition of a B corporation — 'What Are B Corps?' B Lab. <https://www.bcorporation.net/what-are-b-corps>

More people are choosing to become freelancers — Micha Kaufman, 'Five Reasons Half of You Will Be Freelancers in 2020'. *Forbes*, 28 February 2014. <http://www.forbes.com/sites/michakaufman/2014/02/28/five-reasons-half-of-you-will-be-freelancers-in-2020/>

Etsy has 1.5 million sellers — 'About Etsy'. *Etsy.com*, accessed in August 2015. <https://www.etsy.com/about/?ref=ftr>

Etsy is valued at $1.5 billion — 'Etsy, Inc. Stock Quote & Summary Data'. *Nasdaq.com*, accessed in August 2015. <http://www.nasdaq.com/symbol/etsy>

Etsy and the maker movement — 'Artisanal Capitalism: The Art and Craft of Business.' *The Economist,* 4 January 2014. <http://www.economist.com/news/business/21592656-etsy-starting-show-how-maker-movement-can-make-money-art-and-craft-business>

Local and regional food sales —

(1) Jessica Wright, 'Growing Trends in the Local Food Movement Show Industry Is Thriving'. *EcoWatch,* 11 March 2015. <http://ecowatch.com/2015/03/11/local-foods-thriving/>

(2) Sarah Low, et al. 'Trends in U.S. Local and Regional Food Systems: A Report to Congress'. *USDA Economic Research Service,* January 2015. <http://www.ers.usda.gov/publications/ap-administrative-publication/ap-068/report-summary.aspx>

WHO IS RESPONSIBLE FOR SEEING YOUR CUSTOMERS?

'And if you have an area you're working...' — Startup L. Jackson, 'The Counterintuitive Thing About Counterintuitive Things'. <http://startupljackson.com/post/102141918295/the-counterintuitive-thing-about-counterintuitive>

'Every day I'm lucky enough...' — Dylan Blanchard, 'The Best Part of My Job'. *Medium,* 30 October 2013. <https://medium.com/@dylanblanchard/the-best-part-of-my-job-d748ca918232>

If it isn't going to benefit 80 percent... — Dylan Blanchard, in a conversation with Bernadette Jiwa, 2 March 2015.

PART 3: THE OPPORTUNITY WITHIN REACH

'If everyone is busy making everything' — 'Watch: Apple's Poetic Statement On Its Design Process', as transcribed by Mark Wilson. *Fast Company Design,* 13 June 2013. <http://www.fastcodesign.com/1672817/watch-apple-s-poetic-statement-on-its-design-process>

GIVING A DAMN AND THE TRIPLE BOTTOM LINE

'He profits most...' — Arthur F. Sheldon, during remarks at a Rotary convention in 1910. <http://www.quoteland.com/author/Arthur-F-Sheldon-Quotes/1043/>

The Honest Company and the triple bottom line —

(1) Anne Field, 'Jessica Alba: Triple-Bottom-Line Entrepreneur'. *Forbes,* 30 May 2012. <http://www.forbes.com/sites/annefield/2012/05/30/jessica-alba-triple-bottom-line-entrepreneur/>.

(2) Clare O'Connor, 'How Jessica Alba Built a $1 Billion Company, and $200 Million Fortune, Selling Parents Peace of Mind'. *Forbes,* 27 May 2015. <http://www.forbes.com/sites/clareoconnor/2015/05/27/how-jessica-alba-built-a-1-billion-company-and-200-million-fortune-selling-parents-peace-of-mind/>

(3) 'The Honest Company', *Wikipedia.* <http://en.wikipedia.org/wiki/The_Honest_Company>

Origin of the phrase 'triple bottom line' — 'Triple Bottom Line'. *Wikipedia.* <https://en.wikipedia.org/wiki/Triple_bottom_line>

THE CUSTOMER IS YOUR COMPASS

'Code is easy...' — Startup L. Jackson, Twitter (@StartupLJackson), 10 March 2015.

Customers as co-creators — 'Customer-Made,' *Trendwatching.com*, May 2006. <http://trendwatching.com/trends/CUSTOMER-MADE.htm>

Shops as showrooms —

(1) Gopal Kutwaroo, 'From Shops to Showrooms – How Technology Will Save Retail'. *MyCustomer.com*, 4 June 2013. <http://www.mycustomer.com/feature/experience/shops-showrooms-%E2%80%93-how-technology-will-save-retail/164723>

(2) Christopher Thompson, 'Shops Will Be Little More Than Showrooms.' *Financial Times*, 28 October 2012. <http://www.ft.com/cms/s/0/e6ef4454-2122-11e2-babb-00144feabdc0.html#axzz3baJDwJk0>

The Patagonia road trip — 'Worn Wear Spring 2015 Tour—Free Clothing Repairs and More in 15 Cities Across the Country'. *The Cleanest Line*, 6 April 2015. <http://www.thecleanestline.com/2015/04/worn-wear-spring-2015-tour-free-clothing-repairs-and-more.html>

INVISIBLE PROBLEMS

'It's seeing the invisible problem' — Tony Fadell, 'The First Secret of Design Is … Noticing'. TED Talk, March 2015. <http://www.ted.com/talks/tony_fadell_the_first_secret_of_design_is_noticing>

The Apple Watch Short Look feature — David Pierce, 'iPhone Killer: The Secret History of the Apple Watch'. *Wired*. <www.wired.com/2015/04/the-apple-watch/>

30,000 hours of call time — 'A Year in Commerce: A Look Back at Industry Insights, Customer Success, and Shopify Growth'. *Shopify.com*. <http://www.shopify.com/2014>

HARD DATA AND SOFT DATA

'[N]umbers … have the appearance…' — Rory Sutherland, 'Behavioural Economics: What Copywriters Have Always Known but Have Often Found Hard to Explain'. *YouTube*. <https://www.youtube.com/watch?v=0k7RQaQmQcQ>

Information about Velo Cult — The Velo Cult website <http://velocult.com/>

FRICTIONLESS

We can now outsource everything — For examples, see <http://www.redbeacon.com/>, <http://readitfor.me/>, and <https://www.fiverr.com/>.

Trends, shifting expectations, and the on-demand economy — Mary Meeker, *Internet Trends 2015*. KPCB.com, 27 May 2015. <http://kpcbweb2.s3.amazonaws.com/files/90/Internet_Trends_2015.pdf>

Changing screws for the Nest thermostat — Tony Fadell, 'The First Secret of Design Is … Noticing'. TED Talk, March 2015. <http://www.ted.com/talks/tony_fadell_the_first_secret_of_design_is_noticing>

Nest Labs was acquired — Fred Vogelstein, 'Why Google Paid Three Billion Dollars for a Thermostat Company'. *The New Yorker*, 14 January 2014. <http://www.newyorker.com/business/currency/why-google-paid-three-billion-dollars-for-a-thermostat-company>

PART 4: THE STORY STRATEGY BLUEPRINT

'**The successful strategists of the future…**' — Roger Martin, 'Don't Get Blinded by the Numbers'. *Harvard Business Review*, March 2011. <https://hbr.org/2011/03/column-dont-get-blinded-by-the-numbers/ar/1>

WHO IS YOUR MUSE?

Connie Francis and the invention of the keycard —

(1) 'Biography,' *Connie Francis: The Official Site.* <http://www.conniefrancis.com/#!bio4/c1kpq>

(2)   <http://www.assaabloyhospitality.com/en/aah/com/about-us/about-us/our-story/>, 'A Brief History.' Assa Abloy. <http://www.assaabloyhospitality.com/en/aah/com/About-Us/History/>

(3) Assa Abloy ad in *Hotels*, June 2015. <http://library.hotelsmag.com/publication/?i=260510&p=11>

'**So, if I'm going to push my students**' — Linda Cliatt-Wayman, 'How to Fix a Broken School? Lead Fearlessly, Love Hard'. *TEDWomen*, May 2015.   <https://www.ted.com/talks/linda_cliatt_wayman_how_to_fix_a_broken_school_lead_fearlessly_love_hard>

The beginnings of Adidas — 'The Story of Adidas'. *YouTube.* <https://www.youtube.com/watch?v=q55kf_1JNUQ>

'**You're a better designer**' — 'IDEO Partner Fred Dust—Business by Design'. *C2 Montreal,* 21 May 2013. <http://www.c2montreal.com/video/c2mtl-2013-ideo-partner-fred-dust-business-design/>

WORLDVIEWS

'I have older people coming to fitness classes' — Tim Graham, in an email message to Bernadette Jiwa.

CASE STUDIES

'Figure out what matters...' — Evan Williams, 'A Mile Wide, an Inch Deep'. *Medium*, 5 January 2015. <https://medium.com/@ev/a-mile-wide-an-inch-deep-48f36e48d4cb>

SHOES OF PREY

Quotes from Jodie Fox — From an interview with Bernadette Jiwa on 15 December 2014.

Daily customer surveys — Katherine Macpherson, 'How Shoes of Prey Built a Marketing Platform With Social Sharing'. *The Hunter Box*, 25 October 2014. <http://www.thehunterbox.com.au/social-sharing-built-sky-high-marketing-platform-shoes-prey/>

Additional information about Shoes of Prey —

(1) ShoesOfPrey.com <https://www.shoesofprey.com/> <https://www.shoesofprey.com/content/media-release>

(2) Nordstrom press release <http://press.nordstrom.com/phoenix.zhtml?c=211996&p=irol-newsarticle&ID=1990370>

(3) Martine Harte, 'Start Before You're Ready'. *Engaging Women*. <http://engagingwomen.com.au/interviews/jodie-fox-shoes-of-prey/>

(4) Ruth Suehle, 'How Shoes of Prey Lets You Design the Shoe of Your Dreams'. *GeekMom*, 4 June 2013. <http://geekmom.com/2013/06/shoes-of-prey/>

APPBOT

'Surfaces user sentiment…' — Appbot website homepage, accessed in August 2015. <https://appbot.co/>

Additional information about Appbot —

(1) Stuart Hall, 'How We Track Our App Reviews, and Why You Should Too'. Originally published in *Hacker News*; found at *Teknoids* in August 2015. <http://www.teknoids.net/content/how-we-track-our-app-reviews-and-why-you-should-too>

(2) Stuart Hall, 'Lessons Learned Launching a Minimum Viable Product'. *Appbot blog*, 5 September 2012. <http://blog.appbot.co/lessons-learned-launching-a-minimum-viable-product/>

BLACK MILK CLOTHING

Information about Black Milk Clothing —

(1) 'Black Milk Clothing'. <https://www.shopify.com.au/success-stories/black-milk-clothing>

(2) 'About Black Milk Clothing'. <http://blackmilkclothing.com/pages/about-us>

CANVA

Canva 'needed to empower people' — Melanie Perkins, 'How Emotion Helped Grow Our Startup to 2.8M Users in 20 Months'. OnStartups, 1 June 2015. <http://onstartups.com/canva-user-journey>

Additional information about Canva — 'Our Story'. <https://about.canva.com/story/>

FLOW HIVE

Information about Flow Hive; 'we haven't taken all the fun away' — 'Flow Hive: Honey on Tap Directly From Your Beehive'. <https://www.indiegogo.com/projects/flow-hive-honey-on-tap-directly-from-your-beehive>

'Honey on tap'; 'set to work on a decade long task' — 'Flow Hive— Honey on Tap!' <http://www.honeyflow.com/>

'Needs no filtering' — 'How Flow Works'. <http://www.honeyflow.com/about-flow/how-flow-works/p/62>

Set an Indiegogo one-day record — Jessica Harlan, 'Radical Bee Hive Rakes in $4.8 Million'. *Yahoo! Makers,* 10 March 2015. <https://www.yahoo.com/makers/a-sweet-idea-reaps-millions-in-crowdfunding-112910077205.html>

GOPRO

General information about the development of the GoPro —

(1) Ryan Mac, 'The Mad Billionaire Behind GoPro: The World's Hottest Camera Company'. Forbes, 25 March 2013. <http://www.forbes.com/sites/ryanmac/2013/03/04/the-mad-billionaire-behind-gopro-the-worlds-hottest-camera-company/>

(2) 'About Us,' *GoPro.com.* <http://gopro.com/about-us/>

(3) Robert Moritz, 'Guts, Glory, and Megapixels: The Story of GoPro.' *Popular Mechanics*, 12 June 2012. <http://www.popularmechanics.com/adventure/sports/a7703/guts-glory-and-megapixels-the-story-of-gopro-8347639/>

(4) Cool Brands, 'Meeting Nicholas Woodman of GoPro'. *Around the World in 80 Brands.* <https://aroundtheworldin80brands.wordpress.com/2015/01/23/meeting-nicholas-woodman-of-gopro/ >

GoPro was valued at $2.96 billion — Leslie Picker, 'GoPro Jumps After IPO Values Camera Maker at $3 Billion'. *Bloomberg Business*, 26 June 2014. <http://www.bloomberg.com/news/2014-06-25/gopro-raises-427-million-pricing-ipo-at-top-of-marketed-range.html>

LITTLE FLOWERS

Information about Little Flowers — Bernadette Jiwa's interview with Chris Berents, 6 February 2015 and the Little Flowers website. <http://www.littleflowers.com.au/>

KHAN ACADEMY

'The very first time…', 'humanize the classroom', 'global one-world classroom', 'removing the one-size-fits-all lecture', 'penalizes you for experimentation', 'arm teachers with as much data' — Salman Khan, 'Let's Use Video to Reinvent Education.' TED Talk, March 2011. <http://www.ted.com/talks/salman_khan_let_s_use_video_to_reinvent_education>

'A personalized learning resource for all ages' — Khan Academy's About page. <https://www.khanacademy.org/about>

26 million registered students — Khan Academy's Donate page. <https://www.khanacademy.org/donate>

Additional information — Claudia Dreifus, 'It All Started With a 12-Year-Old Cousin.' *The New York Times*, 27 January 2014. <http://www.nytimes.com/2014/01/28/science/salman-khan-turned-family-tutoring-into-khan-academy.html>

HARRY'S

'Andy called him' and 'Andy and I tried every shaving product'
— Jeff Raider, quoted in Scott Bedgood, 'Jeff Raider, Founder of Harry's, Is Always Looking for an Edge.' *ThriveWire.com*, 17 March 2015. <https://thrivewire.com/stories/jeff-raider-founder-of-harrys-is-always-looking-for-an-edge>

Information about Harry's and additional quotes from Jeff Raider

(1) The Harry's website. <https://www.harrys.com/our-story>

(2) 'The Growth Show: Harry's Co-Founder and Co-CEO Jeff Raider'. *Podcast Chart*, 21 July 2015. <http://www.podcastchart.com/podcasts/the-growth-show-8550d0ba-9cd3-495c-9147-ad57095853eb/episodes/harry-s-co-founder-and-co-ceo-jeff-raider>

NIKE FLYEASE

'Out of all the challenges…' — 'Unable to Tie Shoes, a 16-Year-Old With Cerebral Palsy Wrote to Nike. They Came Through Big Time.' *Upworthy.com*, 15 July 2015. <http://www.upworthy.com/unable-to-tie-shoes-a-16-year-old-with-cerebral-palsy-wrote-to-nike-they-came-through-big-time>

A 'wrap-around zipper' — 'The Flyease Journey'. *Nike.com*, 13 July 2015. <http://news.nike.com/news/the-flyease-journey>

CONCLUSION: CLOSE, CLOSER, CLOSEST

'Go out and find some real people' — Tom Kelley and Jonathan Littman, *The Ten Faces of Innovation: IDEO's Strategies for Defeating the Devil's Advocate and Driving Creativity Throughout Your Organization.* (NY: Currency/Doubleday, 2005).

INTENTION AND CERTAINTY

'Ideas are like first dates' — Eric Karjaluoto, 'What's Right in Front of You'. *EricKarjaluoto.com*, 7 April 2014. <http://www.erickarjaluoto.com/blog/whats-right-in-front-of-you/>

A SILVER BULLET OR THE SMALLEST THING

'My mother died when I was two' — Post at *Humans of New York,* 26 August 2015. <http://www.humansofnewyork.com/post/127643269001/my-mother-died-when-i-was-two-years-old-so-its> Also at Instagram: <https://instagram.com/p/607H9jNrLV/?taken-by=humansofny>

SUCCEED WILDLY

'Try not to become' — Albert Einstein quote provided on *Goodreads.com.* <http://www.goodreads.com/quotes/980354-try-not-to-become-a-person-of-success-but-rather>

USING THE STORY STRATEGY BLUEPRINT

'Our task is to read...' — Walter Isaacson, *Steve Jobs.* (NY: Simon & Schuster, 2011).

ACKNOWLEDGEMENTS

Thank you for caring enough about the work you do, the people you lead and the customers you serve to buy a book about creating meaningful ideas.

While a book, like any idea, can be conceived in an instant, anyone who has finished one knows the effort that's involved in breathing life into it. Writing might be a solo endeavour, but publishing a book that you hope will become meaningful to people you care about is a whole other story, and I have a lot of people to thank for bringing this book to you.

I want to acknowledge my three superheroines, Reese Spykerman, Kelly Exeter and Catherine Oliver. The finished product you hold in your hands is a result of their friendship, caring, collaboration, design, editing and love.

Thanks to Seth Godin for inspiring me and countless others to do the thing that is 'too scary to do'. It works every time!

I am lucky to work with, and collide with, the ideas of some incredibly gifted people who set out every day to do meaningful work. Many of these people gave up time to tell me their stories for the book, and some I have never met, but they and their stories inspire me every day. Thanks to James Victore, Brandon Stanton, Cameron Parker,

James Lillis, Ron Johnson, Simon Sinek, Brian Chesky, Jodie Fox, Angela Ahrendts, Scott Belsky, Stuart K. Hall, Dylan Blanchard, Stuart Anderson, Cedar Anderson, Maria Popova, Jeff Raider, Andy Katz-Mayfield, Tina Roth Eisenberg, Nick Woodman, Chris Berents, Sarah Regan, Melanie Perkins, Matthew Walzer, Tobie Hatfield, Salman Khan, Jonathan Ive, Rory Sutherland, Krista Tippett, Dana Marineau, Chris Bruzzo, Karishma Kasabia, Andrew Katkin, Antonio Zea, Andrew Perryman, Mark Dyck, Allison Vesterfelt, Darrell Vesterfelt, Dolores Shore, Charles Cole and Christophe Sut.

To Moyez for unconditional love and to Adam, Kieran and Matthew— the most meaningful work I will ever do.